SIGNPOSTS FOR LIVING

A PSYCHOLOGICAL MANUAL FOR BEING

DR KIRSTEN HUNTER

BOOK 1
**CONTROL YOUR CONSCIOUSNESS –
IN THE DRIVER'S SEAT**

BOOK 2
UNDERSTANDING MYSELF – BE AN EXPERT

BOOK 3
**MINDFULNESS AND STATE OF FLOW –
LIVING WITH PURPOSE AND PASSION**

BOOK 4
**UNDERSTANDING OTHERS –
LOVED ONES TO TRICKY ONES**

BOOK 5
PARENTING – LOVE, PRIDE, APPRENTICESHIP

BOOK 6
NAILING BEING AN ADULT – HAVE THE SKILLS

A MEANINGFUL LIFE

DEVOTE YOURSELF TO:

1. **KNOWING** YOURSELF,

2. **LOVING** OTHERS,

3. **LOVING** YOUR COMMUNITY,

4. **GRATITUDE** FOR THE MOMENT, AND

5. **CREATING SOMETHING** THAT GIVES YOU MEANING AND PURPOSE.

First published 2021 by Kirsten Hunter

Produced by Indie Experts P/L, Australasia
indieexperts.com.au

Copyright © Kirsten Hunter 2021

The moral right of the author to be identified as the author of this work has been asserted.

Except for the purposes of reviewing, no part of this publication may be reproduced or transmitted in any form or by any means, electronic or mechanical, including photocopying, recording or any information storage or retrieval system, without the written permission of the author. Infringers of copyright render themselves viable for prosecution.

Cover design and image by Zach Lawry @ Mates Rates Screen Printing & Design
Edited by Jane Smith @ www.janesmitheditor.com
Internal design by Indie Experts
Typeset in URW DIN by Post Pre-press Group, Brisbane

ISBN 978-1-922742-02-5 (paperback)
ISBN 978-1-922742-03-2 (epub)

Disclaimer: Any information in the book is purely the opinion of the author based on personal experience and should not be taken as business or legal advice. All material is provided for educational purposes only. We recommend to always seek the advice of a qualified professional before making any decision regarding personal and business needs.

To Jon

PREFACE TO THE SERIES

This series of books is actually a conversation that I have had with thousands of people over the last twenty years of clinical psychology work. From approximately 42,000 hours of conversations with clients of all shapes and sizes and from all walks of life, all struggling during their various stages in life, I have learnt so much. When you have the same conversation that many times and you see progress, you see where the value lies. I want to share this conversation with you.

'Signpost for Living' is written out of sheer frustration and exhilaration in equal measure. I have limited hours with my clients. This series of books is the information, across the breadth of 'being human' areas, that I would cover with clients if there was no limit to time. This is my 'ideal situation' series, to share with others how to understand and master ourselves. We are pretty dodgy at being human. We really have very little clue about how we work – we don't fully understand our emotions, our behaviour, our neurology, our physiology – or how to live with purpose, calmness, contentment and joy, with our loved ones and within ourselves. This series covers all of these life-challenge hotspots and things we need to learn about ourselves. If we get support, encouragement, and general guidance in these areas, we can get on track quickly. Life can expand and boom us into more contentment and happiness.

How amazing life is if we allow it to be.

If you get a new puppy, it is wise to put in the time to train it; you can enjoy your pup so much more once it's trained. Your pup becomes easy and fun to walk, reliable on your carpets, and an enjoyable character. This is strangely true for *us* too. By studying our thinking, emotions, behaviour and styles of relating to others – really getting a solid level of self-awareness and having a robust skillset – we can enjoy ourselves and our world so much more. And no, we do *not* need to be puppies to learn new tricks; we can learn as adults, at any stage of life. No excuses here. It is absolutely, profoundly, exasperatingly ridiculous that we do not all learn this information routinely at school. 'How to be human, class 101'. Humans have the code to develop physically, but we need more information to develop psychologically into full adults. Not learning these basic life skills can leave us feeling insecure, disconnected and unsafe.

Life is growth. Life is a work in progress.

This is what these books are about. We do not know everything about 'being human' – far from it – but we do know a fair bit. This knowledge, which comes largely through the profession of psychology, is not, however, common knowledge. And yet it should be. It needs to be. We need a manual for being human, for without it we are driving blind.

This series is based on clinical evidence and sound reasoning. It provides clear, calm direction – not all the answers, but solid signposts. Time to share this knowledge with everyone.

WHAT TO EXPECT IN THE 'SIGNPOSTS FOR LIVING' SERIES

The books in the 'Signposts for Living' series are independent but complementary; by strengthening and cultivating one area you enhance all of the other areas simultaneously. There is not much point fixing one hole in the boat when the other holes are not receiving attention. This is not a piecemeal series. We need to cover the whole of human functioning. In this series there will be chapters you need, chapters you don't, chapters that talk to you now, chapters that will tap you on the shoulder in your future. The 'Signposts for Living' series is written for everyone: all ages, mums and dads, grandparents, young adults and teenagers finding their way.

The books are broken down to first explore (in Book 1) how controlling your consciousness can help you grab the reins to your nervous system, thoughts and emotions. Relevant side-alleys that are common traps to dodgy thinking are included. We then flesh out your personal issues in Book 2: *Understanding Myself*. The importance of being awake in life and aware of your present moment is celebrated in Book 3, along with the gem of living with purpose and passion in a state of flow. 'Signposts for Living' then broadens in Book 4 to discuss understanding our relationships with our people (the good, the bad and the ugly). The true complexity of parenting is then dissected in Book 5. Finally, the art of nailing being an adult is fleshed out in Book 6, revealing the excitement of reaping the rewards of becoming a thriving mature human.

To make the books as concise and user-friendly as possible, I have avoided references, footnotes and other scholarly tools as much as possible. The goal is for you to be able to access and use this valuable information without feeling bogged down or needing to have specialised, background knowledge. To acknowledge my sources and guide you to delve deeper, if you wish to, I have included 'further reading' lists where relevant at the end of each book.

Welcome to understanding your humanness.

BOOK 2
UNDERSTANDING MYSELF –
BE AN EXPERT

CONTENTS

CHAPTER 1	ATTACHMENT FEARS: I AM HERE FOR YOU	1
CHAPTER 2	PROBLEMATIC CHILDHOOD	14
CHAPTER 3	SECONDARY TRAUMA	15
CHAPTER 4	KNOW YOUR HOT ISSUES	17
CHAPTER 5	AGE: HAVE A DEVELOPMENTAL CLUE	23
CHAPTER 6	WHERE ARE OUR RITUALS, RITES AND CUSTOMS?	35
CHAPTER 7	AUTHENTIC SELF – WHO AM I?	38
CHAPTER 8	YOUR VIRTUES, YOUR STRENGTHS OF CHARACTER	52
CHAPTER 9	A CAREER PATH FOR YOU	55
CHAPTER 10	OUR ESSENTIAL FLAWS	58
CHAPTER 11	IMPOSTER SYNDROME	61
CHAPTER 12	SOCIAL MEDIA	63
CHAPTER 13	CONGRUENT SELF = PEACE OF MIND	66
CHAPTER 14	BE PLAYFUL	68
CHAPTER 15	MASCULINE AND FEMININE PARTS OF YOURSELF	70
CHAPTER 16	GRATITUDE	75
CHAPTER 17	HONOURABLE	81
CHAPTER 18	INTROVERT ... EXTROVERT	83
CHAPTER 19	TIME IS YOUR HERO	85
CHAPTER 20	RESILIENCE ... SELF-EFFICACY	87
CHAPTER 21	DEPENDENCIES ... ADDICTIONS	90
CHAPTER 22	SECONDARY GAIN	94

CHAPTER 23	ANGER	96
CHAPTER 24	HOW DOES ANGER MANAGEMENT WORK?	100
CHAPTER 25	SELF-FORGIVENESS ... SELF-COMPASSION	105
CHAPTER 26	ACTIVE RECHARGE, NOT PASSIVE (DRAINING) RECHARGE	110
CHAPTER 27	SLEEP	115
CHAPTER 28	DREAMS	120
CHAPTER 29	HORMONES – TAME THE DRAGON	122
CHAPTER 30	ENERGY TOWARDS OTHERS	124
IN CONCLUSION		126
FURTHER READING		127
ACKNOWLEDGEMENTS		129
ABOUT THE AUTHOR		131

CHAPTER 1
ATTACHMENT FEARS: I AM HERE FOR YOU

Just as numbers and alphabet are the foundations of our education, **attachment** is the foundation of our psychology. And yet the concept of attachment style is not common knowledge. Attachment is the ability to love and to be loved. Apart from our fundamental needs for food, water and shelter, we need to feel secure with key people in our lives. It is important to feel safe. We need to hear and feel from our loved ones, 'I'll be there for you.'

Why do I do what I do?

Our early experiences and our ongoing experiences in life shape how secure we feel in relationships. It is primarily our parental and then partner relationships that play a shaping role, but friendships and family relationships also play a part. Basically, we either feel secure or insecure in our attachment with loved ones. The insecure person fundamentally fears that they are not good enough to be loved, and they fear being abandoned. In response to this fear, they will react in one of two ways: with **anxious insecure** or **avoidant insecure** attachment styles.

As with most things in psychology, your attachment style is on a spectrum. To what degree are you secure, anxious insecure or avoidant insecure? Roughly half the population is securely attached, and half the population is insecurely attached. This means that it is as common to have a problem with attachment as it is to be okay in this area. This high rate of insecure attachment is astonishing; it highlights that the struggle is common. This is sad and unfortunate, but preventable and recoverable.

The following diagram shows the breakdown for attachment styles.

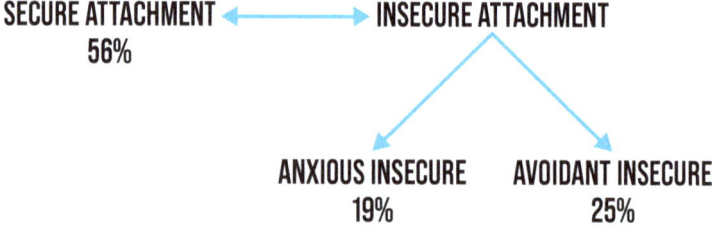

We have the research pioneers John Bowlby and Mary Ainsworth to thank for our knowledge about our attachment needs. This knowledge only came about as a result of a time when we human beings got it very wrong. During World War II, thousands of children were separated from their parents due to the bombing chaos in the United Kingdom, and enormous numbers of children were left orphaned and brought up in parentless institutions. Sadly, this tragic situation allowed us to see the impacts on children when they are separated from their parents and lack that level of parental nurturance. One legacy of World War II was a generation of children who demonstrated anxious and avoidant insecure attachment.

We have since established that our attachment style has a huge influence throughout our lives on our approach to trust and love, and our ability to trust love. We really are driving blind in life if we don't understand our attachment. Our attachment is not just on a conscious level – something that we can just talk ourselves around. Our attachment model is on all levels: conscious, subconscious and unconscious. Attachment is therefore core to our life experience and requires consistent and persevering care if we are to reach a healthy state.

SECURE ATTACHMENT

The secure person is like a puppy dog, light in their presence and ability to be open with loved ones, and open to new relationships. It is relatively easy for them to get close to others and they feel comfortable depending on them and having others depend on them. They don't fear people getting too close to them, and they don't invest energy worrying about being abandoned. They have a light cockiness in their outlook ('You're lucky to be with me'), which says they value and love themselves in a healthy way. They understand that there are no guarantees in life, and they can be let down, abandoned and hurt. But they make an educated gamble that this is not likely to happen – and if it does happen, they feel it is the other person's loss. And while they will feel hurt, they also feel confident that they will ultimately recover and bungee back into life. This bungee back is the resilience that enables us to recover in life.

ANXIOUS INSECURE ATTACHMENT

Anxious insecure people cling; they demand frequent reassurance that they are loved, and evidence that they are a priority. They fear their partner will want to leave them. They feel that others are reluctant to get as close to them as they would like, and they may want to merge completely with their partner. This, of course, can scare people away.

Anxious insecure people seek information that proves their partner's (or friend's) love, believing that with enough reassurance they will feel secure. Sadly, this cannot happen so easily, given that without the template of self-love, we are not able to absorb other people's love. We cannot really believe their messages of love, because we do not believe it is possible.

The anxious insecure person can also set up invisible hoops for their partner to jump through: 'If she loves me she will do this, she will do that.' These hoops are inevitable disasters because of course we cannot impose certain behaviours on another person, and nor should we. They are not performing puppets who behave the way we dictate. They do not need to conform to our prescribed expectations. The anxious insecure person inevitably feels disappointed and greatly hurt when their loved one does not jump through their hoops and prove their love. The good news is that over time, consistent messages and experiences of love can wear the insecure person's defences down and they can gradually learn to feel more secure in receiving love from others.

> *Our loved one cannot fill our bucket with reassurance of their love if we have a hole in our bucket. We must first repair this hole through self-love.*

AVOIDANT INSECURE ATTACHMENT

The avoidant insecure person is a bit of a tricky case. Their logic is, *I've been hurt before, so why would I put myself out there again to be hurt? Do you think I'm an idiot?* This is actually how an anxious insecure person might think also; the difference is just that they are defending themselves by *avoiding* closeness. The avoidant insecure person is working hard to *hide* their anxiety and insecurity.

This is understandable logic in the short term. But we are human, and we need to be loved. So, in the middle to long term, the avoidant insecure person is in a difficult spot: they need people, but they are avoiding letting them in.

The avoidant person hides their vulnerability; they present as confident, perhaps aloof. 'I'm fine.' But they are like a duck on water: above, they are gliding along looking effortless, even confident, but underneath their legs are paddling fast as they try to stay afloat. They fear being hurt again. They fear being vulnerable because if they are hurt again, they don't know if they will recover. They are uncomfortable being close to and trusting others and allowing themselves to depend on others. Their partners often want them to be more intimate and open up to them more. While they look confident, just like the anxious insecure person, they are actually doubting whether they are lovable and valuable to others. When the avoidant person does explore a new relationship, they just put their toe in, and may take a long time to ease into trusting their partner. They can eventually warm up and let a loved one in, or they can remain reserved, keeping a part of themselves 'safe'.

Anxious insecure people are not the same as people who are socialised to be reserved. This reserved group are travelling along in what is normal for them; they engage in light, impersonal conversation and have a stoic approach to problems. Their behaviour is not necessarily based on fear; this is just their cultural norm.

PATHWAYS

With insecure attachment, fear has blocked us from having the relationships that we truly want to have. We can feel panic whenever there is conflict or distance in our romantic lives. We automatically brace ourselves, believing that we are about to be abandoned or abused. While being in love fills us with anxiety, being without love is unbearable. We may notice that these patterns continue to resonate throughout our lives. When we experience insecure attachment, unless we learn about our fears and our patterns and recalibrate our early sense of belonging, we will continue to repeat the same behaviour over and over again. We will continue to feel confused and helpless. We won't understand ourselves. This is about stepping out of Groundhog Day and learning to be loved.

Our attachment style shapes us in how we are with our loved ones from the cradle to the grave. But our working model is not rigid; it continues to be shaped and influenced by positive and negative experiences throughout our life. Our degree of feeling secure or insecure moves around depending on our life experiences. We might start out secure and then have rough teen years with our peers, causing us to become insecure. We might travel well and securely through our child and teen years and then have a critical and oppressive partner who drags us backwards into a state of insecurity.

It's important to know that having insecure attachment as a child does not doom us in our adult relationships. Even if we experience insecure attachment as a child, we can shift this attachment style in adulthood. The good news is that we can recover and claw our way back to a state of security by getting our head healthy, and by having positive relationships that give us a 'corrective experience' through which we can relearn.

The family home is the most powerful structure of human belonging in the world. It is the place where growth, launching, and consolidation occurs. Unfortunately, it is also the place where the most wounds can be inflicted. Wounds that can take a lifetime to heal. The most difficult type of attachment trauma to recover from is the insecure attachment that stems from childhood. This is because our childhood is formative. Children are more able to feel secure, loved and connected if their parents are attuned to the child's internal world of emotional needs. When the parent is attuned to the child, the child feels heard and understood, and this helps the child learn to calm themselves. They also become more skilled and able to connect and engage in empathic, meaningful relationships later in life.

To love and to be loved.

There are so many ways in which parents may fail to meet their child's emotional needs. So many ways we can stuff it up! Parents may be emotionally unavailable because they are preoccupied with their own lives or their relationship struggles. This may cause the child to adapt by dismissing the importance of their own needs, their emotions and their relationships. The child may therefore try not to be dependent on others and may build up a wall as a coping mechanism, believing that they don't need to rely on others.

Or if the parent/s have been inconsistent in their emotional availability and attunement, the child may end up feeling confused and suspicious about how reliable their parents are. The child may grow to develop worries about whether their partner reciprocates their feelings. Being apprehensive about whether others will be reliable and responsive to us may make us reluctant to let others in and to get close with them emotionally and intimately.

If a parent was abusive and frightening, their child's formative years may have been riddled with fear. The child will feel a need to hide, but also want the parent to be there for them and soothe them. This may cause them to grow up into adults who are confused about relationships and their emotions. They may have learnt to be the soother – the one who looks after the needs of the person causing distress – at the expense of their own needs and emotional state.

Unconditional acceptance is extraordinarily important to children. As a child, if our parents threaten to withdraw their love from us when we fail to measure up, then our natural playfulness is gradually replaced by chronic anxiety. Children need to feel that their parents are unconditionally committed to their welfare. This allows them to relax and explore the world without fear. When children feel this way, they don't need to allocate psychological energy to their own protection. Being able to identify the patterns in our history and how they have shaped us puts us on solid footing to move forward and recover from any unhelpful attachment behaviours.

It is difficult to love ourselves if we are not first loved. Our parents and our social environment give us the language to form our understanding of the world. We primarily see the world through this language from our parents. As part of the process of developing, the child asks, 'Who am I?' and, 'How do I feel about myself?' The child starts off largely as a blank canvas and, unfortunately, might have a negative assumption to begin with. ('Maybe I am not okay, not good enough.') The parent's job is to see their child, to hold up a mirror and to reflect back to the child how precious they are, and how their uniqueness and their capability is celebrated.

This external language then becomes internal language for the child over time. It becomes the child's self-talk. This self-talk then becomes the lens for how they see themselves, others and the world, as they launch into the rest of their lives. This is why childhood is so critical to adult development. It is because of this crucial gentle forming of our view of ourselves and the world that we need to be vigilant in protecting children from the uncertainties and the horrors of the world – the adult world.

Our goal is to work towards becoming securely attached, and to develop positive self-talk. To let ourselves understand that we are lovable *because we actually have self-love*. Secure people strive to find a good balance between dependence and independence. The goal is to know that if we are hurt, we feel solid in ourselves – we *know* we will recover if the worst does happen. We can learn that it's healthy to admit when we are upset, and we can try to use our distress to achieve constructive outcomes in our relationships.

The goal is to be grounded enough to take time getting to know our partner and friends, interviewing them, knowing them on a bad day when under stress, being an expert on their ugly side. Only then can we feel confident that we are making an informed decision that this person is trustworthy and adds value to our lives. We then can feel confident that they deserve us. The healing approach is to cultivate a sense of compassion for ourself and understand where our fears have come from. Through controlling our consciousness and understanding our emotions, we can allow the fears to come and go, and experience the freedom to let love in if we choose to do so.

Quality psychological therapy focuses on clients' attachment style. Attachment issues are at the root of most interpersonal problems. Some types of therapy, such as **emotion focused therapy**, work predominantly with the individual's attachment needs. One person might fear criticism from their partner, thinking, *My partner will think I'm not good enough and they might leave me.* The other partner might worry, *My partner is going to cheat on me because I have been cheated on before.*

We develop deeply ingrained habitual ways of interacting with others. You can see why we need to work out what these habitual patterns are if we are going to heal and move forward. We need to understand how the person we are today has been influenced by previous relationships, our early childhood experiences or our other significant adult relationships. We need to respect how our history of connection or disconnection with others has shaped our ability to love and feel loved. This of course links to the 'Know your hot issues' theme in Chapter 4 of this book.

Let's make the point here again: humans have a terrible tendency to repeat old habitual and disastrous patterns. We routinely fear change even when it is clearly good for us. Another sad fact is that many dysfunctional relationships and patterns in life continue because our fear of the unknown is greater than our fear of the unhealthy patterns in our life. So we sit still. We do nothing. We continue to bang our heads on the wall and complain that it hurts. Our challenge is to seek to understand what sets off our reactions, and to expand our awareness and capacity to respond in a healthy, thriving way.

Unless we step back and heal our attachment style, we will repeat our relationship patterns over and over again with different people. We will feel perplexed and helpless about the relentless repetition happening in our lives. But through greater awareness of old patterns that do not serve our health or well-being any longer, we begin to experience a freedom to grow in our capacity, to see new possibilities and to discover new pathways in relating to and loving ourselves and our loved ones. This is about getting unstuck and moving, growing and healing. This all comes from awareness of and then freedom from old patterns. Do we need therapy to achieve this? Perhaps not; we can work through issues ourselves if we have the skills of introspection, and if we have supportive others to discuss our insights and progress with. Does therapy help? Most likely; it can fast track us and it can assist us if we don't quite have the skills or supports to go solo.

CHAPTER 2
PROBLEMATIC CHILDHOOD

It's useful to be aware of how our past has shaped us. An ideal childhood is rare and, ironically, not good for giving us practice for life's future challenges. What is important is that our problematic childhood past is not an excuse to continue with those patterns of behaviour. It's easy to get caught up in defining ourselves by our past hardships and traumas. We can use these as explanations for why our lives are off track. However, we *do* need to take responsibility for how we are *now*. We need to pick up our resources and emotional bruises from our past, and work with these to decide how to approach our future.

CHAPTER 3
SECONDARY TRAUMA

Secondary trauma requires a special mention, as it really interacts with our attachment style and leaves us with pretty horrible emotional shockwaves. Everyone knows what primary trauma is, but few know about secondary trauma, though it is arguably the more damaging of the two.

Here is a confronting example to illustrate: a girl is raped. She comes home to her mum and she says, 'I've been raped.' Her mum responds, 'Are you sure? Wasn't he your boyfriend? Weren't you sexually active? Weren't you drinking? Could it be a misunderstanding?' Or alternatively, the mother says, 'You should have kept yourself safe; you should not have put yourself in that dangerous situation.' The girl is horrified and shocked by her mother's response, her blame, minimisation and even denial. She feels abandoned. In five to ten years' time, the girl heals with regard to the rape to some degree (one hopes), but she does not recover from her mother's lack of support.

When we have an attachment figure, we assume that they are going to be there for us when life gets stressful and traumatic. If this person is not there for us in our time of need, we feel abandonment. Our core sense of security about our world is damaged and disintegrates. This not only damages our relationship with and trust in the person who let us down, but our ability to trust others in the future. By the way, someone off the street – a random person – cannot abandon us. We can only be devastated by abandonment if it comes from someone we have let into our world and trusted, either due to a personal relationship or to their position of authority (like a police officer or a teacher).

Secondary trauma is an issue that comes up frequently in psychology sessions. Another example is a school counsellor who is the primary support person at a school following a student suicide, who then goes on to feel unsupported at the school management level. Or a man who is being physically assaulted by his abusive wife, who is not believed and is even mocked by police. Primary traumas come and go, but secondary traumas hang around. They continue to colour our future intimacy and connection. We learn not to trust our loved ones and/or people in authority because they have proven that they were indeed not trustworthy during our hour of need. This of course all comes back to our primary need of attachment, our need to feel safe and secure in our relationships.

CHAPTER 4
KNOW YOUR HOT ISSUES

We all have our issues and they usually have heat around them – from mild heat to raging thunder. Our issues mess with our life. These are fears that we have formed from our background and lived experience. These are our vulnerable spots, our Achilles heels, that are just sitting there ready to be triggered. We may have a fear of criticism from others because we have those critical thoughts ourselves or have grown up around criticism; we may have a fear of losing our freedom because we have experienced being controlled. We might feel we have to know everything, be the expert, never say sorry, because we grew up without hearing that our loved ones were proud of us. Perhaps being wrong equates to feeling like we are worthless. Perhaps we are not used to our needs having importance. We may have an obsessive need for perfection because otherwise we believe we are a failure. We may blame ourselves for everything because we grew up in the shadows; we may have been brought up being told that we were responsible for others, when really they were responsible for themselves. We may believe that it's only a matter of time before everyone leaves us, because that has been our experience in life on some level or another.

We all have issues. We may have overcome them to a large degree, but we know they are sitting there in our background. And that is okay. This is the vulnerability of being human, and that is the complexity of us as creatures that need each other to form our self-concept and sense of security. The problem is just that we are so fallible, and we often screw up the self-caretaker role.

Our issues come from a melting pot of causes. They may come from our attachment difficulties, or a tendency in our personalities to take things to the extreme (as with perfectionism or catastrophising), or cultural pressures (for example, the success/beauty/image pressures in society). The key is to know what your issues are. Just as we can list off our physical vulnerabilities, we need to be able to list off our psychological vulnerabilities. And just as we look after and even compensate for our physical vulnerabilities or work on strengthening, we need to do the same with our psychological 'hot issues'. Only then can we be proactive in managing them, caring for them and not being ruled by them. We can understand that we are seeing our relationships through the lens of our issues, and then we can work to take these 'issues' glasses off and try to be more objective with our relationships and the situations we are in.

The key is to know what your issues are.

So, what are *your* issues? What are the themes that keep coming up for you in your relationships, in your negative self-talk, in your approach to life choices? What might you be projecting on to others? (Could it be *You will leave me* or *You don't want to know what I think* or *You will be critical of me*?)

List your issues. Literally write them down. Get them out. And keep playing with your list. Keep exploring until you are more of an expert on yourself. This is about being vulnerable. Having the strength and the courage to look at your fears, your weaknesses, your bruises. Many people get lost in the belief that it is best to show a strong façade to the world (and to themselves), but this is not real; it is fiction. The façade crumbles quickly because there is not a strong foundation. To be vulnerable and honest with your issues means being *real* – the actual authentic you. You need courage to find this scary and do it anyway. It means having the genuine strength to be psychologically naked with yourself. From this level of honesty, you can heal, process, spring clean, and strengthen as you become more rational with your history and your role in it. You can then respond with self-compassion. You are arming yourself for your life.

After we have tried to flesh out and know our issues, we then need to spend time working on them and healing. We create our own solution. We can begin to look at them with more analytical distance (as if from a riverbank), rather than thrashing about with them (as explained in

'River of consciousness', Book 1, Chapter 23). Part of this process is defining our issues in words, which in itself will help to gain distance and release from them. Rather than being so focused on the limitations of people around us, we can also take this opportunity to get the 'weeds' out of our own 'garden' first.

It is very good news that whatever our early influences and struggles, we can, through the skill of mindfulness, recognise and validate our experiences and then methodically work through them. After observing and acknowledging our issues, our thoughts and our feelings, we need to use the skills in this book to work through them.

You will inevitably feel some resistance or resentment. This is our defensive wall, our reluctance to look squarely at our thoughts, emotions and behaviours. They are often not flattering. We can even feel self-conscious with ourselves when we are being honest with our issues. They can be confronting. This resistance in itself is information about loaded issues that we carry. It is important to know that resistance is very normal, and working through this level of our reactivity is especially releasing. We must learn from our past if we are to avoid repetitive mistakes and remain trapped in a continual merry-go-round of emotional pain. We have painful memories that need to be worked through; otherwise the pain remains, ferments and grows. Change is the essence of life. It is the goal of all psychotherapeutic conversation.

A commonly held notion is that our future is firmly shaped by our childhood experiences. But there is an ingredient missing here. Us! Our actions, our choices. We reshape ourselves. We are not responsible for what has shaped us, but we are accountable for what we do with it. We need to reject the assumption that even the most awful experiences control and define our lives forever. Our past is gone. We need to accept this reality and work through our past before we can move forward. We are working to feel more secure within ourselves and with others, to learn to be more open and present with our thoughts, feelings and emotions.

This is about strengthening. Through becoming healthier in ourselves we are also able to choose our responses rather than being reactive, and we can become more patient and empathetic with others. This is wisdom. This is the doorway to a healthy regard for yourself and improved relationships with others. For example, we may come to recognise that our experiences as a child are influencing how we are relating and communicating with our partner. This recognition allows us to become more aware of how we react. We can go from avoiding our fears to understanding and working with them. We can then feel more secure and much more connected to our loved ones. This kind of awareness helps us to see our dysfunctional reactions sooner and choose healthier ways of responding sooner. We are soothing the child-learnt reactions; we are letting ourselves know that everything is going to be alright. In truth we are giving parental love and guidance to our child self, to dysfunctional reactions that we took on board when at the time we didn't have any other choice.

CHAPTER 5
AGE: HAVE A DEVELOPMENTAL CLUE

Healthy aging involves development and growth; it means not being stagnant. We need to celebrate the various rites of passage of different age groups, and we need to understand our age so that we can suck the marrow out of every beautiful chapter of life.

We all know about child developmental stages, but what about adult developmental stages? These developmental stages cannot be accelerated or ignored. In fact, they are human life cycles or seasons, and they resonate for generations and reverberate across history. The different cycles of life need to be lived well, as we grow new strengths from them. Throughout our lives we need to take the opportunity to reflect, redirect and re-prioritise ourselves. We need to tweak how we are approaching our relationships, our behaviours, and our lifestyles. We have the constant ability to learn, refine and re-orientate our lives and who we are.

The rhythm of human development.

This chapter is a brief look at the joys and challenges of the broad cycles of adult life, from teenpups to elders. We are better equipped to live life well if we can understand and be prepared for our current age and the next life stage coming towards us, and if we can see how our priorities and our approach to 'making it' in life change over time.

ADOLESCENCE

In adolescence we are dancing between momentous choices and concerns. Which friends, which partner, which job pathway, what do I think of myself, how do people think of me, how do I fit into my family, what do I think of adults in my life? Our development is racing ahead with innumerable areas of challenge and growth. It is a very busy time. Our apprenticeship for adulthood is hands on and can get messy as we try to live in an adult world, but we are still very much childlike in our vulnerability. We are novice adults and we don't like admitting it.

By the time they are seventeen or eighteen, most people have developed sophisticated moral reasoning. They are increasingly able to place negative events in perspective. Their tolerance of frustrations is increasing. The teenager, if given solid parental involvement and role modelling, is starting to be able to control their consciousness. The teenager who has already had bad experiences and outcomes is starting to learn and understand that difficult times do pass; the seas do calm. Time is their friend. Teenagers are (hopefully) sharing their experiences and learning that they are not alone with their concerns and their pain. This knowledge can be very comforting to them.

The younger generation today faces unique challenges. There is a lot of pressure on them to be perfect and successful. Everyone is marketing themselves on social media; it's all about image – the image people want to show the world. It's near impossible for teens and young adults not to compare themselves with or believe in the advertised shiny images of others. It's very, very daunting. The young generation need to know that it's okay to be lost at certain times in their lives.

THE TWENTIES

The twenties is a time of trial and error. We are trying on different ways of living, different groups, different living arrangements, different values and different jobs. Who are we and what are we here for? This is called **identity formation,** and while this stage starts in early adolescence it really ramps up from the ages of twenty-two to twenty-eight. This a time to learn about life and to be adventurous. It is a massive advantage to learn about your own complexity when you are in your twenties. It allows you to explore different life experiences and be aware of different sides of your identity. There is a widening of your experiences and perspective as you add texture to yourself and your life experience. The ultimate goal is to achieve a strong enough sense of self so that when external disappointments come, these hits don't undermine who you are. Learning to have roots in your identity will help to withstand the tough times, the inevitable knocks in life. Ideally we have enough life experience at this time to have learnt what we are really passionate about. It is tricky that many choose their university study area before they have really worked out their adult selves and their passions.

Part of the refining of life skills is learning not to be too erratic when stressed – too reactive, too blunt, too competitive, too submissive. Adults in their twenties are learning how crucial it is to be mindful of others in their interactions. They are learning how to communicate in more sophisticated ways; they are practising adapting their communication styles to elicit a good response. Only by refining these skills can we work collaboratively without triggering each other's egos and defensiveness. We learn by getting this wrong and then (hopefully!) by getting it right.

MAGIC TWENTY-EIGHT

The age of twenty-eight gets its own shout-out because it is the age where we reach real adulthood psychologically. We now have fully developed adult brains and we are past the messy younger twenties stage. By the age of twenty-eight we have perhaps achieved the work of identity formation. This is a great time to have confidence that who you are now will likely be who you will be in the future. Your self-identity has stabilised to a large degree.

Prior to twenty-eight, we are not only changing and experimenting with who we are, but we also do not have the full maturity to understand that things change – that *we* will change. We will have completely different interests, perspectives and preferences as we progress through each of our age stages. It is for this reason that we need to consider carefully any choices we make in our early twenties that will have long-lasting consequences.

Take tattoos, for example. When we get a tattoo, we are making an estimation that we will like this image on our body for the rest of our lives. But getting a permanent tattoo at a young age does not speak to your future self; it only speaks to your adolescent or young adult self. Imagine if you had to pick a shirt to wear for the rest of your life – say when you are thirty-seven, fifty-seven, seventy-seven and ninety-seven years old. I think you'd realise that you would become bored with that shirt and would probably not have the same taste in clothes at ninety-seven that you had at twenty-seven. Why then do we not get this concept with permanent ink? I am not in any way against tattoos; I'm just pretty exhausted with talking to people who in their thirties already regret their tattoos. This regret will likely only get stronger with age. So perhaps with tattoos – or other major life-changing decisions – hold off till you're twenty-eight. Your call.

OUR PRIME: THIRTY TO FIFTY-FOUR

For many people the years from thirty to fifty-four are perhaps the first point of reflection and evaluation in their lives.

By then we have accumulated some life experiences, we are growing our knowledge of ourselves and others, and we can stop and have times of introspection. Sometimes this might be brought on by feeling like we are at some kind of crossroad. From our life experience and age, our emotions can now stabilise with less intensity. Our highs are not as high, and our lows are usually not as low.

Life roles can change a lot during this stage. New mothers often find they lose their own identity and life pursuits, given the demanding task of parenting. New fathers can find that they are no longer number one to their spouses, but number two after their children. During our lives we can review stages and decide to make changes to our priorities and relationships with others. Our life pathways and who we have become may not be in tune with those of old friends, and we may move apart. You may decide to look differently – through your new value system – at family relationships that you have always just fallen in with in the past. You may shift boundaries. At this point, many choose to distance themselves.

There can be a sense of urgency: 'I'm getting older; if I don't make it soon, I might not make it at all.' There can be a sense that we need to be 'successful' by a certain age. Men and women often need to decide whether to pour excessive time into their careers or optimise time with their children. We can feel torn; we can feel the tension between the ambitious career world and the child-nurturing home world. We have previously had a desire to grow up. This desire had now been realised and released, and we now focus on staying young and sometimes living young. Our perspective goes from grasping for the future to wanting to consolidate and slow down our world, and find contentment and pleasure. We are yearning for a greater meaning in life than the superficial distractions that can shape our twenties. We are looking for self-expression, compassion, creativity, and a deeper connection with our world.

We are starting to come into our prime. Our knowledge, our life wisdom, and our capacity to take responsibility and steer our lives is coming to the point where we may have full maturity. Only when we have a strong sense of who we are and a capacity to find confidence from within and not from the external world can we reach our prime. It is the substance of us that matters and gives us joy and peace. Physical beauty is lovely and can continue through life. But it is so important to understand that there are many versions of beauty, not just the generic cookie-cutter version of beauty that the media tells our seventeen-year-olds to aspire to. Nothing is more beautiful than someone who radiates a vivacious joy and contentment in life.

LIFE-MATURED AND SEASONED ADULTS: FIFTY-FIVE TO SEVENTY-FOUR YEARS

From fifty-five to seventy-four, the world will want us to be old. People may make assumptions of us and try to pigeonhole us, but this is the age in which living in a spirited way keeps us young. It is our outlook that either keeps us young or ages us, not our bodies.

Age is something to be celebrated. With age we become freer of social pressure and convention, we have a wealth of life experience and wisdom about ourselves, the world and interpersonal relationships. We have had time to figure out who we are and what matters to us. This is a time to look for creativity to keep us young; we need to stay open to fresh new experiences, activities, people, projects and adventures. It is a time for continuing to experiment with life, growth and self-expression. Continuing to expand who we are is the key to living with spirit. We need to keep busy living and having a playful approach to life. We also need to keep our physical connection with others at this age; hugs connect us, massage soothes us. Don't lose touch with the need to receive this connection physically.

The question of retirement is interesting. Basically, we need to consider how to retire from work but not from our passions. This is a problem if our sole passion, purpose and role in life is our work role. It is extraordinarily crucial, if you are a workaholic, to get solid roots established in passions outside of your work role *before* you retire from work. Otherwise, you will retire from work and feel completely lost in your identity, your world and your purpose. You are likely to have significant adjustment and grief issues, with a danger of spiralling into depression and acceleration of aging. The key to continuing to have a youthful outlook and momentum in life is continuing to honour and make time for your passions. You might need to be creative here to work out how to apply them in a different context. Some early planning and action can really help you to transition to and enjoy this next phase of your life.

Keeping with this theme, but jumping to the next age group, let me tell you about a dear friend of mine – an eighty-one-year-old psychologist whose passion is learning. She goes to all of the professional development events that I wish I could get to; she is alive with childlike curiosity and learning. She is contagious in her passion. Another example is a ninety-one-year-old gentleman who had a passion for breeding birds. He loved it; it was his pleasure and his routine; the birds were part of his family, and caring for them kept him moving and vital; he was in good form. His family pressured him to sell his birds, as they wanted him to take it easy. With the selling of his birds, he lost his life momentum and purpose, he lost his light, then aged quickly and died. The answer: never retire from life.

When you look at a lot of Asian cultures you see this golden rule in full spirit. At sunrise in Singapore, for example, the streets are busy with very elderly people going for their walks before the heat of the day. They then continue in the roles they have always played, contributing to the family business and the routines that nurture the family. We can learn a lot here. You are as young as you feel. If you feel this purpose and momentum, no one can take this youthfulness away from you.

> *You don't stop doing things because you get old.*
> *You get old because you stop doing things.*
> Rosamunde Pilcher, writer

It is often in these years that women who, after years of nurturing everyone else, can finally look after their own individual needs. Just as traditionally some men cannot let go of their work roles, some women are somewhat addicted to their role of providing for and organising their loved ones. They can't stop, and the idea of letting go is scary. They often feel lost and disorientated. They don't know how to focus on themselves, how to put down tools and *be*, rather than *do*. They need to learn that they can love their family by 'being with' them, rather than through their previous role of 'doing for' their family. This is how they need to learn to express their care and love during these years.

Our culture does not value the attraction of life-matured folk; we are busy worshipping youthful beauty. It is therefore hard for us to feel desirable and confident when wanting to meet potential partners in this age group. We fear dating and intimacy – which is ridiculous, because most likely we are searching for someone else who is of a similar age, so our age prejudice against ourselves is hypocritical. Many are so fearful that they choose loneliness over the fear of rejection. It is too scary to put ourselves out there, to take a risk.

THE ELDERS OF OUR TRIBE: SEVENTY-FIVE YEARS ONWARDS

The community is truly grounded and made rich from this generational group. They are our role models, our inspiration. They have refined their life skills to have a true connection with the rhythms of time, nature and ancestry, and the greater themes of humanity are usually important to them. In previous eras and in some cultures still, the elders of the tribe were or are honoured, cared for with tenderness and considered great value to the community. Our present-day Western world emphasises image superficiality, a speeding rat-race world, and individualism rather than family- or community-mindedness. This has led to a pattern of overlooking the older generation. Not drawing on the knowledge and considered opinions of folk from this generation is foolish. Their holistic, historical and experienced perspective is a resource that needs to be revered, embraced and savoured.

It is time to address the devalued state of the elderly. Although it is on the cards that there will be some deterioration of mind and body with age, there *are* important strengths remaining, and we don't celebrate or prize them enough. If we gradually feel devalued as we become older, then we may feel diminished in our lives. This is a problem and leads to all sorts of issues. The elderly are our historians; they have lived in time capsules that younger generations have not. They have knowledge, experience and perspectives that can broaden world views and teach valuable lessons. Their stories will go with them, so we need to take the time to sit and be in the moment with them – listening, not talking.

Many elderly people feel invisible; they feel – and probably are – ignored. They feel like they are a burden, an obligation. While many of the elderly do need a lot of time and support from their families, there is grave danger that they will be pigeonholed as time-consuming dependants. Even though they may require care and support, this needs to be balanced by a reverence for what they also bring to our worlds. They are the elders of the tribe, and if they earnt our respect during their prime years, then this respect needs to continue.

CHAPTER 6
WHERE ARE OUR RITUALS, RITES AND CUSTOMS?

Rituals, rites and customs were and are used to mark and celebrate major changes in life: our life milestones and our connections with people, place and history. They encourage us to reflect on the meaning of what is occurring. In our Western world, however, we are frequently lost in our 'racing through life' mentality. Our high-paced, pressured worlds have us focusing on and worrying about what comes next. We have forgotten how to navigate and mark out different phases of life. We have forgotten to recognise that others have passed this way before. We are missing out on the calming force of feeling that we are part of something bigger than ourselves, and have become disrespectful and ignorant of our sacred passages.

It is important to stop and acknowledge and celebrate our experience of life stages. This is us being present in our lives. Rites of passage occur at all ages and enable us to take a broad view of life. We know that we only remember a sliver of our history. We are very selective about what we hold on to in our memories and make part of our life story. We remember events – weddings, funerals, graduations, coming-of-age celebrations, religious events – but not so much daily life. That's why life rituals help us remember life. Perhaps this is one reason why we have celebratory rituals?

These life passages may involve entering a committed relationship; changing career; having children; seeing our children start school and our teenagers having their first truly adult role by living independently or travelling; adopting a healthy and mindful approach to health; attending reunions; buying our first house; separating from a dysfunctional relationship; putting in boundaries to protect ourselves from a previous unhealthy relationship; adjusting to a chronic health condition; or going on a trip planned for many years. They are milestones of accomplishment and personal growth: life. Bringing together our loved ones and our community to celebrate our future direction and to acknowledge our past is the obvious form of ritual.

Rituals represent a stage of change; you are shedding the skin of your previous identity and emerging in your next life stage. This is a separation from your previous, normal way of living, and it can be scary and confusing as you try something new. You then face a time of growth and re-integrating in this new stage of expansion with your life. While you continue to allow yourself to emerge, stay flexible with the sense of who you are and take the time to work it out. *Still* yourself; don't distract yourself with busyness. These life transitions are about flexibility to change, letting go of our previous 'normal' and often our previous sense of control. We often need to lose ourselves in order to forge a new self.

You may be working out a new way to live your life. This stage of change can be very scary. People don't tolerate confusion, ambiguity, uncertainty and unsettled emotion very well. Rather than understanding and respecting this process and the need for change and growth, we often tend to think there is something wrong. We might also blame and take our troubles out on loved ones. We need to be brave during this transition and understand the enormous opportunities that are before us. Missing out on possibilities available to us is like missing out on living.

CHAPTER 7
AUTHENTIC SELF – WHO AM I?

As well as our relationship with our loved ones and our sense of purpose, the most vital relationship in life is with ourselves. This is our understanding of who we are as our own individual, and how we feel about ourselves. This is the foundation relationship upon which other relationships in our world depend. If we neglect our relationship with ourselves, then we become dependent on our external world for reassurance, identity and acceptance. Without this self-love, we look for love from the outer world in all the wrong places. We can step out and live in the world with strength only through having a robust relationship with ourselves.

Our pursuit of a strong relationship with ourselves is a solo expedition. We have to go on a continued adventure, a quest to learn about ourselves and ground ourselves in self-compassion, contentment and gratitude. This involves solitude, introspection and long periods of quietness within ourselves. These are lessons and experiences that involve internal realisations – working towards waking up and comprehending life's truths and the shortness of life. It can be scary and painful. When we do connect and become intimate with ourselves, however, we expand; we become larger in ourselves and we embrace change because we understand that this is essential growth. We become more open to what life can offer us, we become more touched by life, and we realise that barriers to a better life are not only from outside ourselves. It is up to us to create the life that we want to live.

Here is the thing about self-worth: it just *is*.

Compare it with the love for a child. When a child is born, we inherently value and cherish that child. The baby cannot 'do' anything; it is not at birth demonstrating how intelligent, athletic, artistic, or charismatic it will be. Wonderfully, we have unconditional love for that child. Our love is not conditional on the child's capacity for anything. The child has inherent value for us. Full stop. The child is like gold. We value the precious metal; it does not matter what shape it is formed into, for the core value of that precious metal remains the same.

So too with us; it is not what we are doing, or how we are doing it, or how we look, or what we own that creates our value. Our value is inherent. No hoops to jump through, no shapes to contort to create our value; we just *are* of value. This is our self-worth.

We have unconditional love for our children. We need to have the same unconditional love for ourselves. We need to be awake so we can love the core of ourselves. Our love is not based on our expectations of ourselves. With this unconditional love for ourselves we can then feel secure to go forward and live into our potential. It is not living to our potential that brings self-love; it is the other way around. Unconditional self-love is our starting block in life. There is no room for negative self-talk when it comes to self-love; negative self-talk is having *conditional* love for ourselves.

When we start as a baby we are perfect in our purity. We are then bombarded with others, and affected by their insecurities and their neglect, and by society's cultural flaws. We are then consumed by misguided self-reflection. We start to question, 'Am I okay?' This implies, 'I might not be okay'. And before long, our ego gets in the way and our insecurities have us questioning ourselves. We put up walls to try to protect our vulnerability and impress others or intimidate others. We humans make a messy business of developing our self-identity and our authentic self.

The good news is that we can learn our patterns and recover and grow into a healthier version of ourselves and our approach to our lives.

Your sense of your inner beauty – the unique fingerprint of who you are – is a very private thing. If you view yourself through the lens of others, then you will just be seeing *their* stuff, *their* issues and *their* reactivity. Your own inner beauty will become distorted and blurred. Your sense of self is a private conversation; it is not open to the public. Nobody can teach me who I am. You can describe parts of me, but who I am and what I need – these are things I have to find out myself. We need to be our own inner architects that keep reviewing the design of who we are. This is the pathway of learning to 'know thyself'.

When we reduce it down, the process of finding who you are is really about discovering that the miracle is life itself. It is the miracle of living each moment being true to ourselves. 'Be here now' – the idea of living each moment true to yourself – is contrary to our culture, which sees our worth in terms of *becoming* something, *doing* something, *proving* our self-worth. But you are already something: you are yourself. The authentic self is about acceptance of yourself, and this acceptance brings peace.

Trust yourself.

You need to live your own life. It is impossible to become like somebody else. You need to be open and receptive to learning over time who you are, and living your own life, moment by moment. The outside pressure for us to live and chase others' expectations and act according to the world's agenda means that we can get trapped on the world's mouse wheel of *doing*, rather than living our own lives.

We learn to defer to authorities in how we see ourselves. Proclamations are made about us. Parents tell us whether we are well behaved or not; our art is assessed by our teachers as good or not; our report cards tell us we are smart or not; our coach tells us if we made the cut or not; doctors tell us if we are healthy or not. Social media also has us jumping through hoops for acceptance and the desire to have the image that others set out for us. Not fitting into what social media tells us we should be can have us at the depths of despair and can result in problems like eating disorders.

When connecting with our own self, we really need to step off the social media grid. We have to decide that nobody is going to tell us who we are. We are seeking a sense of belonging, and then unfortunately we get seduced by a desire to fit the social media template of acceptance. The outcome of course is that we lose our expression of ourselves and gain an inevitable sense of inadequacy.

Our authentic self requires that we live our lives in our own way, not conforming to the demands that we fit into certain moulds. Rather, being authentic means that we live a life that reflects our identity and our priorities. This is not about being purely self-focused; indeed our love for our family, friends and community is usually at the core of the true richness in our lives. Being authentic means being awake to our personalised approach to our lives. This is one of the advantages of travelling. We can often have some time to connect with ourselves and come back with a fresh head and a fresh approach to our lives, honouring what is important to us. The key is to keep this fresh review mode and not to slip back into old patterns and the rat race of life.

Part of having a healthy and buoyant sense of self is to practise loving kindness towards yourself. This means that just as you care for others, you care for yourself. This loving kindness soothes your sense of feeling overwhelmed by your fears and your stresses. Love and compassion towards yourself and others releases the negative emotions of resentment, jealousy, greed, and hatred.

By practising loving kindness towards ourselves, we become less egocentric. We create a genuine lightness in our being through having more space in our mind and freedom from our emotions. Caring for self is the top priority on our to-do list, as it is the fuel that allows us to do everything else on the list. You fill the car with gas before you go off to do all your other things. Loving kindness toward yourself is your fuel. It is essential. You may think that it is indulgent, that you do not deserve this self-care. But caring for the self is not only rational and founded, it is pragmatic and sensible, and you will be better for yourself and others as a result.

We need to playfully experiment with what we find meaningful and brings us joy. This can be whimsical and freeing. It is not about what other people find enjoyable;

it is about what *you* find enjoyable. Working out what you don't like is part of working yourself out and celebrating your unique self. I personally can't stand hens' nights and those parties where people sell domestic products. I don't like being a passenger in a group car trip; I don't like smorgasbords or just lying by a pool. 'Funniest videos' where people get hurt or upset annoy me (a lot!). My childhood has put me off cricket and cars. Often at social events, I would rather be at home with my family or a good book. And oh, pet peeve: I can't stand those party whistles; they make me just want to crawl into the ground.

There is nothing wrong with any of the above – they are just not for me. It is okay to be different; uniqueness is to be celebrated. It is what makes you the individual that you are. Practise your power of choice and learn to trust your decisions, not because they have to be right, but because, on balance, that seems to be where you are sitting with the issue in that moment. We don't need firm and forever answers; we just need an experimental openness. No pressure, no big deal. Of course, the other part to the equation that we then continue to experiment with is working out what we *do* enjoy, and to embrace the weirdness of our uniqueness as it unfolds.

To find yourself, think for yourself.
Socrates, Greek philosopher

A lot of our troubles and the world's troubles stem from lack of self-image – from not being confident in who you are and what you're supposed to be doing in life. We often react through our insecurity. To further cope with and hide this insecurity we front up with our defensive mask, trying tirelessly to feel less vulnerable. The goal is to become good friends with ourselves. It is vital to like yourself, to have faith in yourself. To be connected to your healthy family and friends who strengthen and celebrate you.

A classic sign of insecurity is the inability to receive praise from others. Without having self-love and self-appreciation, we do not have the template within ourselves to receive praise from others. We do not believe the praise; we don't know what to do with it and it makes us uncomfortable. It is important to fill our lives with things that help us grow and help us sleep with contentment and peace of mind. To deepen our sense of who we are, we have to accept that this process involves continued subtle change and growth. We need to capture the parts of us that have passion, delight and creativity. Living well is a gesture of faith in ourselves and our truest possibilities, the extent of which are always unknown.

I've tried to fit moulds, rather than being me.
Alice, twenty-four-year-old client

Here is an intriguing link: our self-esteem can be traced back to prehistoric times. As discussed in Book 1: *Control your consciousness*, humanity was first purely focused on physical survival. Our primal brain, led by our amygdala, made sure that we were focused on searching for danger in our environment, and having fight/flight/faint/freeze responses. Then we moved to being verbal while living in tribes. Our search for danger then became also related to the tribe. Because we were living amongst our tribe, we needed to work alongside them; we needed to get on so that the other members didn't stab us in our sleep. We asked ourselves, 'Am I okay with my tribe?', 'Am I fitting in?', 'What do they think of me?' Our survival depended on getting on with our tribe.

This theme has continued to the present day. We have 'ingroup' and 'outgroup' tendencies. Groups tend to select someone to be on the 'out'. This is comforting for the other members because it means another person is on the 'out', and by contrast, *they* are on the 'in' of the group. It is very difficult for the group to hold together and not have someone on the 'out'. This person can become the black sheep, and within the group dynamics, being different can equal being wrong.

All shapes and sizes of families have experienced this 'black sheep' dynamic. A family of engineering-type people might have an artistic child who does not fit into their mould. The artistic child is often therefore cast as the black sheep. Conversely, a creative anti-establishment family may have a child who wants to pursue law and is conservative in her outlook. They are confounded and cannot relate, making this child the black sheep. A family with a long line of tradies who stay close to home don't know what to do with their travelling, alternative aunty – cue the black sheep. We get comfortable with our 'normal' and can be inflexible to differences, and, more importantly, we can use this difference to select the member who will be on the 'out'. Embracing our individuality is difficult if we know we're going to get persecuted for it.

Interesting question: what portion of the world's interpersonal problems come down to insecurity about self worth? I would argue the majority. Imagine – if we could give a confidence dose to everyone in the world, how many of our issues would fall away. What would this do to someone who bitches? They would not have as much need to be critical of others, because they woud not be feeling threatened by comparisons with themselves. We would be able to become more 'other-person' orientated, because we would be feeling more fuelled up within ourselves. We would not have the need to control others, because we would not have as intense a fear of being out of control. We would not rely on all the status props to define and feel good about ourselves. The world's materialism would settle. On a global level, we would not be thinking as much about ourselves, and we would be more mindful of our disastrous footprint. The business world's elite might take on a whole new approach, making decisions that primarily support the people and the planet, not themselves.

WHEN?

Many of us wait to know who we are. But this approach misses the point. We are *always* learning who we are. Self-identity is a constant process, not a destination we finally arrive at. We can't get the job done of 'finding myself' and then just park ourselves for life. We always need movement and growth; otherwise we have stagnation. We would be trapped if we did not grow. We are always building our own world. Rather than asking ourselves, 'Who am I?', we need a constant curiosity to enjoy the question of 'Who am I at this point?' which is based on continued learning about ourselves. Don't wait until you know who you are. You are always learning who you are. It is more a case of 'This is where I am right now, and this is the direction that I want to take at this point in life'. Life is an innovative art in which we continue to undergo a process of reinvention of who we are. Awareness of ourselves and our patterns is needed for this flexible way of approaching our life.

Be yourself. Ultimately just be yourself.

Some of the key ways to continue to form our identity – our authentic self – are:

1. When you look at art, listen to music or see some architecture, focus on what *you* think of it, rather than what others tell you to think. While you may respect

the skill that went into something, you do not have to like it, even if it is priceless. Tapping into your artistic or creative side gives you direct permission for personal expression. We need to practise building our strength to have our own voice. It is not important to impose this voice on others; what matters is tapping into the voice within ourselves. We continue to find out who we are by experimenting with our opinions, preferences, values and lifestyle. We constantly learn what we think and feel about things, and what makes us feel recharged and well within ourselves. Nobody is born with their voice or their personal approach; we are constantly learning.

2. Learn to tolerate uncertainty and continue to be flexible in exploring life. 'I'm not really sure who I am, so I will remain open to what comes along in life and learn how I respond.' This openness is helpful in allowing us to broaden ourselves and absorb more of a rich tapestry as our identity forms through our life.

3. Find a positive identity through achievement. Finding what we are good at, or what gives us a sense of accomplishment and meaning is nourishing for our sense of ourselves. It is important, however, to remain open to all the other parts of ourselves and our other areas of exploration; otherwise our area of achievement can actually trap us and hedge us in. We do not want to narrow our lives. Our areas of achievement can instead be a solid anchor point for our other areas

of exploration and growth. Achievements are forward moving and they can tap into creative expression. They can help build relationships and strength and can make your world and the world for others around you better.

4. Learn to overcome the anxiety of not knowing who you are. Our continued possibilities always remain unknown until we reach a crossroads with new experiences in life. Rather than relaxing into the gentle forming of our identity, and trusting time and the gradual growth process, many of us feel confused, anxious and rushed. We want reassurance of the end result. This is pure anxiety speaking, and it really makes no sense as we will never arrive at our final identity formation anyway. Ideally, we are always growing and expanding. Sorry for the cliché, but it *is* literally the journey, not the destination, that matters when it comes to our identity formation. So try to relax and enjoy the ride. Enjoy what you have figured out so far, and enjoy your continual learning, tweaking, growth and self-discovery.

5. Beware of thinking, *This is it; this is all I can be; this is all I expect from life.* A tendency to resign from our identity formation is very dangerous, and we can create a depressive prison for ourselves if we decide that we are going to stand still and clip our wings. This can put out the fire of passions and dreams. In resigning like this, rather than being a thriving adult, many turn to

self-medicating with drugs, alcohol or gambling to escape living. We need to choose love and life, not an anaesthetised approach to life. We need to build our lives so that they are large enough to encompass our dreams.

Gaining the gift of being yourself involves sifting the trivial from the essential in your approach to living. By doing this we can be precisely who we are and who we want to be. When we are no longer trying to live in the shadow of others, our envy melts away and confidence becomes natural to us.

> You were created with intrinsic value.
> You are a unique creation.
> Your body is a miracle.
> See your value, open your eyes.

CHAPTER 8
YOUR VIRTUES, YOUR STRENGTHS OF CHARACTER

We all have personal virtues or strengths of character – our personal strengths that we bring to the table and live through. Through these strengths of character, we continue to grow and expand. These are moral traits, not talents like academic ability, beauty, or athletic speed. The reason we prize people as our role models is usually because they clearly epitomise these strengths of character. We then follow their example as we consolidate our own strengths of character. Hard times are when our strengths of character can really come to the fore. Adults who lived through World War II, now known as the 'Greatest Generation', faced their troubles with character strengths that saw them forge through and manage extraordinary times of stress.

Be as you wish to seem.
Socrates, Greek philosopher

What are the different strengths of character? Here we turn to psychologist Martin Seligman, who has researched this area in depth. He found that across the world's religions and philosophical traditions, stretching over 3000 years – from the Old Testament and the Talmud to Aristotle and Plato, Confucius, Aquinas and Augustine, Buddha, the Koran, Lao-Tze, Benjamin Franklin, the Upanishads, and Bushido (the samurai code) – there are six virtues in common. Almost all religions and philosophical traditions endorse these six virtues as being core to strength of character. They are:

1. Wisdom and knowledge
2. Courage
3. Love and humanity
4. Justice
5. Temperance (self-restraint)
6. Spirituality and transcendence.

Our personal strengths are our resources to get through life and also our way to find many of the state of flow activities that sustain us (coming up in Book 5). It is therefore our goal in life to develop our strengths of character and to use them in all areas of our lives – with family, relationships, parenting, work, friendships, finding purpose and living well. We can reflect on where we sit with each of these strengths of character, and then work to make them even stronger. We also need to mindfully buffer against areas that we know are our weaknesses. There are no shortcuts to this depth of living, and neither should there be.

Strengths of character can be built and strengthened over time with clear awareness, practice and dedication. It is our choice to build and use these strengths of character in our daily life. This is about ownership, creation and discovery. This is where having role models and parents with positive strengths of character is so helpful. Our strengths of character are, of course, in line with our personal value system and expression of ourselves.

Strengths of character really come through when we think about the kind of personal legacy we want to leave with our loved ones. How can you act in a way that shows the world and your loved ones how to live? There are so many deeper rewards that ripple out from focusing on expanding and cementing our character strengths. For example, a deep sense of humility through spirituality allows us to dodge around the demands of our own ego. With these strengths of character, we can attach ourselves to something larger than us in our value system. While pleasures soothe and tantalise your sensations in the moment, a meaningful life needs to look beyond.

CHAPTER 9
A CAREER PATH FOR YOU

It is important that with all of our best intentions, we do not pressure our children to choose the career path that makes sense to us. It is their life and they need to choose something that will match their needs, not ours. If they choose their career path to please their parent, then they are not living their own life; they are living their parent's life.

We cannot have them fearing disappointing their parents or feeling judged by their parents. We cannot presume to know what our child will ultimately enjoy. Instead we need to give our child their voice, to *see* our child and *listen to* them. This is their creative expression of their work selves, their own interests, aptitudes and aspirations. If we cast them as a black sheep for not being an accountant, a businessperson, a doctor, a tradie, or an artist, they will live with resentment towards us and we will be missing the best part of them. It is staggering how many adult clients share this problem as their story. It is very sad to inherently clash with the nature of your job but feel too invested or financially trapped to change.

> We need to give our child their voice,
> to *see* our child and *listen* to them.

It is *your* life you are living, and nobody else's. Find out who you are and find out what you really believe in. Pay careful attention to finding out what you feel attracted to and where you feel uncomfortable. Do whatever comes best to you. Each person must discover where they want to put their energy. Through trial and error, we work through our options to choose the path that gives us purpose and fits with our strengths. The reflection required to steer our path requires us to be in touch with our own experience. We need to be in the habit of reflection to decide our course of action. When our goals are well chosen, we are more prepared to have courage in pursuing them despite hurdles and opposition. When we are living with authentic goals, we have a reason to wake and we are more likely to wake feeling good, which is a wonderful thing. The way that your passions and talents influence you is part of their power, and it will serve to respect them. If you stifle and smother these passions then you will live feeling discontented, as if you are limping along. You need to dream and work towards visions of yourself and your future.

Let's be clear: it's the *meaning* of your work that matters, it is not about high-flying prestige. Some people who thrive on order and streamlined systems are most contented when they are doing administrative work away from the public. Others love being part of a team, love feeling needed and having constant fresh tasks and fresh faces; they may love, for example, being a hospital warden. I know swimming instructors who are light-years more contented with their work than many lawyers and doctors I know. This is about finding your fit, not society's perception of that fit. You have to listen very closely to who you are.

It is a smart idea to choose your profession based on what you are drawn to. What do you want to read, look at, watch a documentary about, learn and talk about? What does your brain naturally process easily and comprehensively? Just notice what you are drawn to. If you choose well, hopefully you will have a sense that your profession is not a job but something that you find meaning in and enjoy doing. It is what helps us wake up feeling good in the morning and happy to go to work. Finding a work area or profession that reflects your strengths and interests is a wonderful thing.

CHAPTER 10
OUR ESSENTIAL FLAWS

At a funeral, what is it that touches our hearts about the person we are reflecting on? While we celebrate their accomplishments, it is their quirks and their harmless limitations that warm our memories and make us smile. These flaws are what make us unique and warmly human.

We are all flawed. It is strange when people pressure themselves to be a perfect version of themselves. We think, *I'll be a good version of myself if I change my weight, my income, my laugh, my wrinkles, my home.* But we are not supposed to be perfect. We are human, not robots; that is the point. We do not need to be cardboard cut-outs of some version of someone else, and we are not perfect puppets controlled by the world's expectations. The word 'perfect' does not apply to humans; it applies to mathematics: 1 + 1 = 2. Our flaws often incorporate the most lovable parts of ourselves. I'm talking about our gentle flaws here, of course: our idiosyncrasies. I am not talking about flaws that cross the line and hurt others.

It is important for our family and friends to let us know that it is okay for us to be ourselves, and that they love and accept us with all of our uniqueness and our weirdness.

Perhaps all of us have odd traits: our family history, our ears, our voice, our hair, our stutter, our people skills, our learning capacity, our ability to connect, our relationship history, our harmless fetishes, our obsessive tendencies, our travelling quirks, our home routines, our food preferences. I could literally list a hundred areas. It is our job to figure this out, learn to be confident despite our flaws, incorporate them, work with them. That is part of our uniqueness, our weirdness.

We all have our weirdness. We do not need to get it *right* or be tidy in ourselves. What matters is accepting and celebrating our weirdness. There's not only one weird thing about us; there are many. The magic is to have a sense of humour about our weirdness and to find our path. We are experiencing a healthy process of maturation when we allow ourselves to internalise the understanding that we are uniquely valuable. We can then have a stable sense of ourselves. When our vulnerable self shows our weirdness to our significant other, *this* is intimacy. This is letting them in.

The truth is that we are the result of a lot of accidents of birth. We don't get to choose our gifts, our athleticism, our intelligence, our looks, our height, our metabolism, our aptitude, our natural interpersonal traits, where we are born or to whom, our access to education and health care, our family's level of functioning. We don't get to choose anything on this launching level. *Our only real choice is to be us.*

Some of the most unhappy and frustrated people are those who can't come to grips with who they are. Our aim is to accept and embrace ourselves, warts and all, and then grow, expand and move forward. Either we come to grips with who we are, or we go a bit nuts and live in a constant state of frustration with ourselves. We need to get on board with ourselves. Contentment is in no way a reflection of the world we have around us; it is our attitude, our acceptance, and our gratitude for what we have.

We do not need to hide our flaws or parts of ourselves from our safe people. Our flaws stem from the hardest parts of our life. But these dark times, when we have needed courage, often ultimately end up being times of growth and strengthening. These challenging times require us to be prepared for unexpected opportunities, and to understand that life is mysterious and messy. We can develop the ability to cope with – even embrace – this uncertainty. This is the skill of formulating new goals, rather than wasting our energy on inner turmoil. These are our times of facing fears with courage and discovering our power. Without difficult times we do not discover our power.

Our gentle flaws require us to practise loving acceptance and a sense of humour with ourselves. We need to be proud of who we are, flaws and all, and live our truth.

CHAPTER 11
IMPOSTER SYNDROME

Imposter syndrome is the tendency to be unable to internalise accomplishments. We just can't believe that we are capable of performing at that level, or worthy of being promoted to our new level. We feel inadequate. We feel like we have been faking our way to where we have come, and sooner or later people will realise.

Some people who are experienced in their roles continue to experience imposter syndrome. They have negative self-talk that perpetually undervalues their strengths. Many people experience imposter syndrome during the long process of finding their feet in a new role, whether this be as a parent, partner or in a work role. We don't realise that while we have not yet completely mastered all of the skills that we need, we are clearly showing a capacity to achieve what we are achieving. We don't realise that it is normal to not feel comfortable in our new role until we have had a lot of practice and exposure. We need 'muscle memory' in our roles in order to feel that we belong and feel comfortable in our role, and this takes time. It is normal to feel daunted while things are new, and in fact a lot of people around us are 'faking it till they make it' also. Meanwhile we feel like a fraud, pretending to play the role that we are in. We need to be patient with the process of adjustment and realise that it is normal. There is not necessarily a problem with our performance; it is just that we have not had the time or exposure to feel confident in our role yet.

Breathe; wait until it is all not new anymore, and *then* look around and see how you feel.

CHAPTER 12
SOCIAL MEDIA

I need you to ask yourself a question, and you want to give yourself a truly honest answer. Look deep; look into your honest truth. If you are on social media, why? Is it for approval from others, an attempt to be what you think others want you to be? Are you looking for validation? So many people make their private lives a product that they market. They self-promote, trying to seduce others with a particular (and selective) version of their lives.

We can easily become dependent on social media as a hollow and empty source of approval. Many are constantly striving to make others admire them. How is that working for us? A modern-day spike in depression and anxiety – a feeling of being lost – is the result. It is dangerous to absorb everyone else's energy. The reality is that authenticity is a very private conversation with ourselves that involves no one else's eyes or input. It is quietly personal – between you and yourself. We do not need to buy into the trending culture. We can think and act for ourselves.

I recall a couple separating. The wife posted a photo of them sitting on top of a mountain looking out at the sunset. It was beautiful and it looked like an ideal romantic moment, true intimacy. The husband showed me the uploaded photo and he was furious. The photo was actually taken in a moment of intense conflict, when they were deciding to separate. To add another layer, their teenage son had taken the photo with no clue that his parents were in that moment separating. The wife was so consumed by wanting to portray her personal life in an idealistic way that she posted a very painful moment to social media. In this action, she was profoundly insensitive to her husband, her son and to her own personal story.

Social media often circles around largely superficial values: looks and wealth as a portrayal of success. When someone has pure goodwill there is rarely self-promotion involved. A true core value system needs no audience. It is the opinion of people within our intimate circle that we should care about: our loved ones, family and friends. Decisions should not be based on self-promotion. Indeed, the beauty of our private life is precious, so perhaps this privacy should be closely held? Intimate and personal conversations and information should belong in the intimate circle. My beautiful husband Jon once articulated that humbleness means allowing other people to discover our virtues through their experience of us. The exact opposite of self-promotion through social media.

UNPLUG: I DARE YOU

Choose to have one day per week when screens are off – TV and internet. Two days would quadruple the impact. Discover how addicted you are. Unplug. Find out what it is like to be human for a bit, without being catered for by immediate stimulation and gratification. Plug purely into thoughts and actions that come from within you, as opposed to plugging into the world where you are being cued and prompted and told what you should think and crave.

The old Amish order, who live in a way consistent with the eighteenth-century pre-technology era, have one-tenth the rate of depression as non-Amish Americans. It is no surprise that depression is most prevalent in wealthy nations, for we are losing ourselves in the hollow superficiality that the media promotes. Just have a holiday off the grid. I bet you the best things in your life only happen when you are truly present. If unplugging from the grid is hard for you to do, then you need to do it.

CHAPTER 13
CONGRUENT SELF = PEACE OF MIND

Congruence is consistency in ourselves and harmony with the person that we are. We each have an *ideal self* which embodies how we want to be, encompassing our higher values. And we have our *actual self*: the true summary of who we are, day in and day out – how we behave, think and feel. When there is a good overlap between our ideal self and our actual self, we are congruent within ourselves. We have peace of mind. We are content and thriving by living in a way that is true to our values.

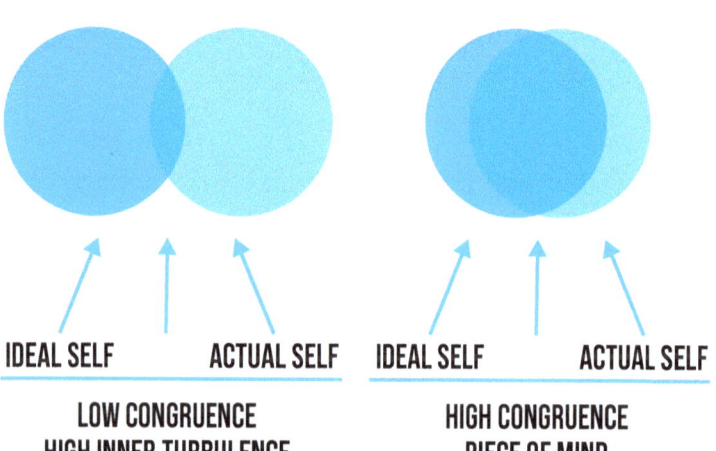

IDEAL SELF   ACTUAL SELF   IDEAL SELF   ACTUAL SELF

LOW CONGRUENCE   HIGH CONGRUENCE
HIGH INNER TURBULENCE   PIECE OF MIND

This peace of mind is literally priceless. It is living well. If there is a separation between our ideal self and our actual self, we are in turbulence; we are far from proud and content with ourselves. This can be torturous. Work towards living by your values; be honest, have integrity and be in a state of growth. I feel genuine compassion for people who are seduced into a life of self-absorption and moral corruption, as they have no peace of mind.

CHAPTER 14
BE PLAYFUL

Mental health involves playfulness and joy in living. This means being absorbed in our sense of purpose and our enjoyment of the here and now. Being playful is about extracting intense and varied fun from life and being the child who is lost in wonderment. If we approach challenges with dedication and a sense of responsibility but also playfulness, suddenly we don't experience our challenges with such anxiety. We have lightened up. Yes, we have to be serious about our standards in how we treat others and ourselves (our self-talk, our health, our financial security). But we really don't have to be in a serious mode when we try new things, experiment, risk failure, have financial wants, and flirt with status pressure. Confidence means being able to regard yourself with good humour, and being okay with being goofy sometimes.

When we appreciate the absurd, unpredictable, quirkiness of human life we can delight in ourselves and others. We can learn not to take life too seriously and we can become grounded. Laughter is the sound of freedom. Enjoy inexplicable occurrences. Look for the funny side of life; it is the antidote to our ego. Through humour we can have great compassion for the dilemmas and perplexities of life as they are thrown at us. We will also approach these obstacles with more inner calm and therefore a dramatic increase in inner resources. At the minimum, we won't sabotage ourselves with self-imposed anxiety. Much of life is a game.

Don't take yourself too seriously. You can take your profession and your love for others seriously, but not yourself. We are only a small part of the big circus out there. If you take yourself too seriously you will paralyse your creativity and your instincts, and you might sabotage yourself with self-doubt and pressure. Also, if you are light and confident in your approach to things, life usually comes off for you. People are drawn to your ease and your lightness in being.

CHAPTER 15
MASCULINE AND FEMININE PARTS OF YOURSELF

There is more in common than there are differences between the genders. This should unite us. This should help us cut through the crap of thousands of years of ignorant gender carry-on. But we have a way to go there. When we look at gender expressions at each end of the continuum of masculinity and femininity, there are distinct differences that need to be celebrated, embraced and actively benefited from. To be clear, this is not about gender, this is about embracing your individuality. Our femininity and masculinity is separate from our gender. This is about reflecting on your own personal levels of femininity and masculinity, and working out which dynamics and issues apply to you.

We humans all have inner 'masculine' and inner 'feminine' aspects or parts. Their co-existence is like a dance between our strength and our tenderness. Both are essential and both balance us. Our masculine parts involve our determination, drive, and energy. Our feminine parts include our gentleness, our caring, loving and creative sides, and our community-mindedness. Men and women have both masculine and feminine parts; they are not gender exclusive. This is why men and women have more in common than we have differences. To reach a well-rounded and mature self-identity, we need to meld together the two forces of our inner masculine and feminine aspects of ourselves. This expands us into the potential of who we are.

The power and strength of the masculine can have the negative influence of making us inflexible and hard if it is not counterbalanced by our inner feminine side, which allows us to connect with others and see the world outside of our ego. Our feminine side has us defining success through our degree of connectedness and relationships, while masculinity bases the definition of success more on accomplishments. Think of our teen years. The teen girl often wants to know 'Do you like me? Am I part of the group?' and she focuses on fear of relationship exclusion. Teen boys, while they still want to be included, are often more concerned with 'Do you respect me?' Their conversations are often about their skill level or knowledge level about all sorts of random things, or their capacity to carry humour. For both genders, these are years during which we're either searching for or setting down our anchor points for confidence and positive self-talk.

Interestingly, women may be more acquainted with the feminine nurturing cyclic nature of life, as they themselves experience the cycle of menstruation and pregnancy. They experience these cycles of life first-hand, in their person. Often young men only discover their inner feminine selves when they first fall in love. They have lived with male camaraderie and are used to being in action mode. They have not spent much time reflecting on their own inner selves or on intimate connection, intimacy and communication. Through love they can experience the powerful mix of sensitivity and willpower and strength within themselves.

Research has found that depression and anxiety are more common in women than in men. Women also, however, experience considerably more frequent and intense positive and negative emotion than men. Does this difference lie in biology, or in women being more willing to report and perhaps admit to experiencing strong emotion?

Young men need to slip out from their mothers' warm care and embrace to become men, and a good dose of masculinity helps here. The unkind label of a 'mummy's boy' has been penned to describe when it appears to others that this transition into adult masculinity has not been mastered. The young man needs to learn to embrace his challenges in life rather than shy away. During this time of transition to manhood, an older, wiser male role model can help the young man to access his compassion and sense of justice.

As adults, when men lose touch with their feminine side, they are likely to become interpersonally isolated, lonely and moody. They overemphasise their drive to compete. Financial and career success can feel hollow as they hide a home life that is short of love, joy and connection. Such a man has learnt to live for himself and his ego, not his loved ones. He says that he works for his family, but he is not part of the family, and his family do not want financial or success glory from him. They want their dad and their husband. What matters are the *people* in his life, but these core relationships have often been neglected. This situation is a ticking time bomb. Divorce rates are extremely high when there is such a high level of interpersonal disconnection and neglect on the home front. His physical health may also be at significant risk.

Young women need to access and embrace their masculinity; otherwise they may be prone to anxiety and disorganised in themselves and their future direction. Our masculine energies allow us to access our strength and power, our decisive action, mastery and independence. It is crucial, however, for women not to lose their femininity when embracing their masculinity. Being a feminist is not about becoming masculine; it is about embracing the females' worth and rights. We don't want femininity to dominate masculinity, or masculinity to dominate feminity. The point is celebration and valuing of both genders as equals. The ability to use the feminine and masculine sides of ourselves is powerful and supports us as we develop resilience and feelings of belonging.

Our goal is to remain flexible and adaptive in our ability to relate to the world by calling on both our feminine and masculine parts, and we need a good dose of both. Why call on only half of our strengths? We fly with two wings, not one. We need to embrace and integrate our strength and action (masculine) side with our (feminine) capacity for connection, emotion and creative play.

Too many people do not identify the masculine and feminine aspects of themselves. They do not take responsibility for the integration of these parts and they frequently expect their partners to make up for masculine or feminine deficiencies within themselves. This leads to relationships in which the individuals are not fully developed. The man may become increasingly Neanderthal, aggressive, dominant and ineffective with others, and the female may become increasingly reliant, dependent and vulnerable. We cannot remedy flaws in each other, and any compensation we make for our partner is only short term as we become worn down and resentful towards them.

Society has historically valued masculine traits – short-term achievement over sustainability, achievement over collaboration, individualism over community – but there is a shift on the horizon. The current generation of teens through to those in their thirties are especially passionate and vocal about interpersonal connection, communication, environmental ethics, and authentic goals. I feel very positive about the empowered and, hopefully, more rounded values of the emerging generations.

CHAPTER 16
GRATITUDE

Gratitude is about being awake to the amazing, wonderful things in our lives and events around us, both big and small. It is the opposite to sleepwalking through life and getting caught on life's paralysing treadmill. It is even acknowledging that death will come, so that we value life now. When we take a few minutes every day to reflect on the good stuff that is happening in our lives, we create a bridge that allows us to realise that many of our goals are actually already being fulfilled. We pause and look around – and that simple act creates congruence within us. We acknowledge what is going well and what is gelling for us, and we can swim in the synchronicity of our lives.

If we don't stop and recognise our moments, they pass by, lost in the greyness of our memories. This is about feeling good through appreciation for what is in front of us. If we do not open our eyes and see the beauty and the joy, then what is the point of having these positives in our lives?

What a wonderful life I've had!
I only wish I'd realized it sooner.
Colette, novelist

Our brains only have so much capacity for attention. We can choose to focus on positive or negative components with this finite attention span. You have two pathways to choose from: the grateful pathway where the hypothalamus is stimulated to regulate your anxiety, or the anxious pathway where the amygdala is fired up and leading the charge. How do *you* want to live? Do you look to the beauty or the darkness? Do you expand or contract?

Be careful here, because habits and patterns repeat. **Confirmation bias** is a tendency to look for information that proves what we expect to see or confirms what we already believe to be true. It means paying selective attention to the world around us.

When you look for the beauty in life, savouring all those minuscule or grand moments, then your brain will look for even more things around you to be grateful for. But the reverse is also true. Just as with **negative attribution style** (discussed in Book 4, Chapter 7), when we expect problems, loss and disaster, we will search for them until we find them. One of my favourite authors, John O'Donohue, whom I cite throughout this book, explains it beautifully in his book *Beauty: the invisible embrace*: 'When our eyes are graced with wonder, the world reveals its wonders to us. There are people who see only dullness in the world and that is because their eyes have already been dulled. So much depends on how we look at things. The quality of our looking determines what we come to see.'

If you want to feel contentment, serenity and satisfaction, the essential ingredients are gratitude, appreciation and an ability to savour the good in your life, past, present and future. Without gratitude as a strength in your life, it does not matter what good fortune and blessings you have, you will miss them. It's like having your eyes closed.

We need to appreciate that our bodies are truly miraculous. Every day we live in a functioning miracle and we take it for granted. This is one aspect of loving yourself: it is seeing the miracle of what you have to work with, and loving your body. To be a friend to yourself – to be a support to yourself rather than an opponent and a bully – you need to see the features of yourself that you value and cherish. Be yourself, love yourself, and have gratitude for who you are.

And what of the world around us? We are surrounded by abundant beauties and pleasures and we fail to see them. Why? Because they are always there, they are not novel. We focus on novelty and look for novelty. There is a level of greed in not knowing how to find contentment with our worlds but instead looking for novel pursuits in the hope they will make us happy.

> *Gratitude is not only the greatest of virtues, but the parent of all others.*
> Cicero, Roman philosopher

How do we bring gratitude to our lives, past, present and future? Our attitude to our memories creates our relationship with our past. Focus on finding aspects of your past in which you were blessed. Have gratitude for all of the things you would have missed if you had not had them (for example, your home, your family, your friends, your capacity to do all the daily things you so routinely can do, your access to music, entertainment, conversation, nutritious food – you name it).

Gratitude amplifies the appreciation of previous events and allows us to savour them. We can rewrite history through gratitude, unlocking and releasing bitterness about our past. Think about when you had hard times to master, and think of how they made you grow and strengthen. We can appreciate the silver lining from our painful chapters. This can defuse the toxic effect of rigid grudges. Whether we feel contentment or bitterness, pride or shame, our relationship with our memories shapes our relationship with ourselves now. Gratitude plays a crucial role here as it shapes how we feel about our past, and therefore how we feel about ourselves. Gratitude increases our life satisfaction as it amplifies our good memories about our past. Rather than dissecting and finding the negative, we can look with value for all of the good fortune that came along the way.

By doing this, the intensity and frequency of our positive memories are encoded and they become our story. More positive thoughts will come to mind – the good things, the blessings – and we feel contentment and happiness.

Consider a simple example where a family goes for a holiday. The person lacking in gratitude will focus on the effort to pack, the constant attention required for the children, the occasional tensions that form. The person with gratitude will acknowledge those challenges but understand that they are par for the course. The grateful person thinks of how blessed they were to have a large family, to be able to get away, to have good health, to have blue-skied weather and wild nature to absorb. They would feel gratitude for the change of pace and the space to follow their nose and have gentle pleasure time alone and, preciously, together. They would enjoy the laughter, the silly stories that become family stories, and the bonding. They understand that this holiday will be remembered in time as a window of specialness, and if they had stayed home, then that time might have been unremarkable and held no long-term memories.

Have gratitude for *now* – for finding a carpark, for having a decent shopping centre in the first place (hence the need to look for a park!), for our child's smile, for our friends' funny stories, for our joy of reading, for the delicate or comforting tastes of our dinner. This absolutely overlaps with mindfulness and living in the present.

> *He is a wise man who does not grieve for the things which he is not, but rather rejoices for those which he has.*
> Epictetus, Greek philosopher

The last area for gratitude is the future. We as humans need a horizon to swim towards. We need to feel hopeful about the future and we need to feel empowered (not hopeless) to move towards this future. We need to feel that on some level we have some capacity to work towards our goals. Depression is learned hopelessness and learned helplessness. It is this perspective of a positive and empowered outlook for our future that is a cornerstone for mental health. This is a sense of gratitude that we have the resources and capacity that we do have, and that we can formulate goals for the future and work towards them.

CHAPTER 17
HONOURABLE

Be honourable, have integrity and be true to your word. Honour is not an old-fashioned concept. People need to be able to rely on your word. Otherwise your words won't mean anything, and your relationships will dissolve from lack of trust. This is about you deserving and gaining the respect of others. This is about your actions leading to others holding you in high regard. This is about acting with integrity. What greater compliment is there than being known for your integrity? It is of course not always easy to act in a way that is aligned with your values. We all make life mistakes and go off-track. The key is owning our role and responsibility and working hard to grow and get it right next time. This insight, ownership and growth allow us to maintain our integrity. We do not need to be perfect to maintain our integrity. What matters is our genuine intention.

> *Honour is about deserving and gaining the respect of others.*

A smart and effective way to support us on our path is to have role models who embody integrity. We can look to them to model our code of conduct. They will give us inspiration and show us that acting with integrity is doable. When in a tricky situation, we might find guidance about the way forward by asking ourselves, 'What would (name) do?' We can also merge the positive aspects of all of our role models together, so that they create a sense of who we want to be in the world.

CHAPTER 18
INTROVERT ... EXTROVERT

How do you recharge? With or without people? How does being with people affect you? How much time do you need with your tribe? We are talking about your level of **introversion** or **extroversion** here. Introversion and extroversion are on a continuum, and you sit somewhere along it.

EXTREME	MILD	MILD	EXTREME
INTROVERSION		EXTROVERSION	

Introverts recharge their energy on their own. They can enjoy people but there is a point at which they start to feel drained and need time to themselves to recharge. After they have had this time on their own, they are then ready to reconnect with people again. An extrovert recharges by being with people. When they are with people they refuel and become more and more energised. They leave the party because it is over, not because they feel they need to. They look for social contact not only because they enjoy it, but because it gives them a boost. Time alone is okay, but they could not live in an isolated situation. They need to be with people to get their equilibrium back and re-boost their energy. This time might be with a partner or with their children; it does not need to be in an outside social environment.

It is important not to get introversion and extroversion confused with shyness and outgoingness. You can be a shy extrovert or an outgoing introvert. This can be tricky because the shy extrovert has to overcome their shyness to connect with others, especially if they do not have family and friends they can readily access. In creating a robust social network, their shyness can be a significant hurdle. Also, many people assume that shy people don't need social contact, and wrongly assume they are introverted. By the same token, outgoing introverts are often misunderstood. They present as confident and highly social, so many assume they are extroverts. People may not understand that they can only take so much social contact and that they need to retreat to recuperate and recharge their energy. This is interestingly often the case with comedians.

Once we know our balance, we can work with our needs. It is important not to rigidly pigeonhole ourselves. An extrovert still needs time to themselves and can have a people-saturation point, and an introvert can have too much of their own company. If you know your general tendency and recharge orientation, you can self-care and be mindful to seek your energy refuel with or without people.

CHAPTER 19
TIME IS YOUR HERO

Time passes. That is a guarantee in life. We really don't focus enough on the amazing resource that time is. When dealing with acute stress and pain, it is time that we can look to. The acuteness will subside over time, and we will move through our crisis point. Appreciating time can boost our morale. If we only looked to the gift of time.

An example of how we can do this is journalling. If we write down our stressors during acute times then later look back on them, we soon notice that our written recounts have lost relevance to us. We don't necessarily continue to hold the same opinions or intensity of emotion. Our life has moved on to a different focus, and stressors have moved on in one way or another. It is a sign of wisdom when we can put our stressors in perspective as we are experiencing them. If we realise that 'this too shall pass'.

This too shall pass.

Our awareness that time passes also motivates us to stop and savour our experiences, our people and our moments while they are with us. If we were to calculate how much time (minutes and hours) in our lives we are going to spend with a loved one based on our previous frequency of contact, we may be surprised that it is actually not a lot. If we remain aware that we have finite time with each other, we can then wake up and create and embrace our moments together.

Remember, no human condition is ever permanent. Then you will not be overjoyed in good fortune, nor too scornful in misfortune.

Socrates, Greek philosopher

I have a beautiful mother. I'm very fortunate, and we are very close. As with all people and all relationships, we get annoyed with each other at times. When, inevitably, her little quirks irritate me, I work to not let myself get annoyed. I tell myself that these are things I'm really going to miss when she's not here, so I strangely enjoy them now. Sounds odd, but it's true. When we appreciate time, we appreciate the positive and even negative things in life with acuity.

CHAPTER 20
RESILIENCE ...
SELF-EFFICACY

In our teens and early twenties we often set out with a plan for our life, a sketch from A to B, so that we can be successful in what we do. But this is not life. Life has curves and ditches. You cannot choreograph life. Life is not smooth; it is messy. Living well means getting through difficult times, having the self-belief that you can do it, and strengthening through them. This means building and drawing on our resilience. **Resilience** is the ability to bungee back, during and after tough times in life. It is recovery. It is the ability to respond with flexibility, taking in different perspectives of the problem, and calling upon a range of inner resources to deal with challenges we face. We embrace our past and use resilience to transform and build our lives. Our sense of humour can truly be developed through tough times.

Self-efficacy is belief that you can do what you need to do. It is training yourself to see your own potential and your own power. It is about having faith in yourself. Resilience and self-efficacy align. Our ultimate approach when we are truly mastering life's tough times is to view adversity as a challenge, to find satisfaction in understanding, managing and recovering from hard times. It is definitely a skill to make the best of our difficult times and to see them as times to learn and grow. It is great to let our teenagers know that they are going to have challenging times in their lives and (ever the theme) that life is messy. The message being: 'Try not to do any real harm on the way, make sure you learn and strengthen through life, and I am here to support you through your difficult times and your adventures.'

My life has been anything but linear. One reason I think I am a half-decent psychologist is that I have been through many challenging chapters and not just survived but grown and built in personal awareness, strength and skills. Adversity has been my friend. And I have no regrets, not in the scheme of things. If I had regrets and wished for my life path to have been different from what it has been, then I would not have the people in my life that I have today and I wouldn't be the person that I am. While I would not want to experience them again, I am strangely grateful for the hard times.

We are generally not celebrating, however, when we're in the middle of our difficult life crossroads. It takes time, distance from the event, and strengthening from the experience to have gratitude for our hard times. It is these difficult times that help us put down strong roots and makes us capable of weathering future storms. It is from this root system that we grow, and this that gives us a strong foundation. We can then broaden in our capacity; we can grow a bigger canopy for life and cast a bigger positive shadow of influence in our world.

The struggle that a butterfly has to get out of its cocoon is part of the process of strengthening that it needs in order to fly. We cannot help a butterfly emerge from its chrysalis. If we were impatient with this natural process and helped the butterfly, it would not be able to fly. It is exactly this breaking out of the chrysalis that builds the butterfly's strength to fly. Sometimes life cannot be hurried. Life is often the boot camp that we need to become psychologically fit and healthy for later life. The key is to know how to learn through these life experiences. Our struggles are important. They forge our character, our life skills and our self-awareness. It is only through struggles that we become strong and resilient. This is stress hardiness and it becomes a protective factor in our ability to cope with our future struggles.

CHAPTER 21
DEPENDENCIES ... ADDICTIONS

Dependencies or addictions are largely unconscious coping strategies that we use to numb ourselves from our stressors, or to try to create a false sense of control. They do not work, however, and they do not actually help us to overcome our problems. Instead they damage us and leave us in a deeper, darker hole. With dependencies we just go in circles and stagnate. We do not conquer our problems, learn or grow. Some dependencies are substance abuse, smoking, obsessive cleaning, obsessive busyness, workaholism, compulsive social media use, compulsive retail spending and compulsive sexual behaviours. Dependencies are about relieving ourselves of our responsibility to address problems; we become a passenger to our problems, and are in avoidance mode. We are keeping our minds from facing depressing thoughts.

In the long term, dependencies lead to psychological and physical breakdown. And a lot of these dependencies are socially normal, even expected. It is as if, because everyone is doing it, it must be okay. But to give in to these socially accepted dependencies is just to join the hordes that are also living in 'escape mode' and going in circles. Being common does not mean it is healthy.

An example is male social drinking in rural Australia. At pubs or events, many men routinely drink themselves blind. To not join in with their peers means to face social exclusion. While their children, their partners, their mental and physical health are suffering –and often to a point of collapse – the option of not joining their peers at the pub seems impossible. A healthy relationship with alcohol for a rural Australian male can be social suicide.

The healthy alternative to a dependency involves acknowledging our emotional state rather than suppressing it, and developing tools for working with our stressors. This learning to respond to stress mindfully helps us to gradually move away from our old dependencies. This is like bringing light to our darkness, and awareness to our mindless reactions. Once we are familiar and practised with our healthy alternatives, we can choose them more skillfully. If dependency was our previous coping style as a bridge over our stress, then we need to build a new healthy bridge – a stronger bridge, made of self-knowledge and many solid skills; it is then that we can offer ourselves another way of living, another way of getting through.

While fear can be an effective motivator in the short term to move us out of our dependent cycles of behaviour, it is usually not useful in producing lasting change. Fear can be an ingredient, but we really need a positive desire to live well, an ambition to care for ourselves, and self-respect. This gives us a positive force for change, rather than the negative and short-term force of fear.

To overcome a dependency, we need to replace it with many other habits and life skills that are our new way of coping and living. You cannot take away one wheel from a car and not replace it with another. While dependency has been a damaging wheel, it has been how the person has been managing to exist and cope with life. This new replacement way of living has to have many threads to it, so that when one positive approach is not working, there is a wealth of other healthy living habits to fall back on. This is the key to stopping the cycle of relapsing into previous dependent behaviour.

So, when we are stressed, we might call on any of our top five healthy coping mechanisms. Some suggestions are to go for a walk, write in a journal, call a friend, listen to music that lifts our mood, have a shower, read a book, or just go outside and absorb the world around us. And when we reach for people, we need several to reach for so that our success rate is fairly solid. While the responsibility for change falls 100% with us, our support crew is really important for our morale and to make us feel supported. We must treat our loved ones with love and respect if they are to stay by our side to support us. They have a duty of care to themselves not to be abused, and we cannot have them harmed while we are ourselves recovering.

We need movement and growth to overcome dependency. We need to be working towards several short-term, mid-term and long-term goals that really excite us and guide us away from old habits. We need to be creating happy and healthy daily routines and rituals that are an investment into our self-care and self-respect. These are choices that make us feel better afterwards. Drinking a lot of water, daily stretching and exercise (even if it is just a walk around the block), and eating in a way that you are proud of shows self-care. These are all the threads that come together to create the rope that pulls you out of the depths and the clawing grasp of dependencies. It absolutely can be done.

We also need to be realistic about relapse. Relapse happens, yes. Relapse is almost an inevitable fact while overcoming dependencies. The key is to push through until the relapses stop happening. Then you have broken your old coping mould. Dependency can be the adversity that we grow and launch from. The dark times of dependency can be the harsh life lessons that develop us into humans with wonderful depth and breadth of life experience. No regrets when there is ownership and growth. This will be the time when you needed to think bravely of your life in a new way. It takes courage and determination – the opposite to the passivity of dependency.

CHAPTER 22
SECONDARY GAIN

Quick chat on **secondary gain**. What is it? It is an invisible force that keeps us stuck in unhealthy patterns. Secondary gain means that we have learnt to get some benefit from our problems. Basically, sometimes we get into a habit of being defined by our problems; they become like a comfortable pair of shoes. Or we learn that our problems help us gain attention from people in our worlds, whether positive or negative. We can therefore stop wanting to help ourselves; we choose the stagnant way of living rather than finding recovery and growth. While we may verbally complain, our actions say we are strangely content and comfortable with sitting in our own mess.

Someone who keeps damaging their relationships because they like the drama or the power is experiencing secondary gain. Another example is someone who enjoys illness because the attention makes them feel special (with an extreme example being hypochondriasis). Or someone who stays in their bad situation because they are so fearful of change. Or the person with the martyr complex, who plays the role of the reluctant doer and carer for others and doesn't know how to stop. Or our disability might have become part of our identity, the way that we think of ourselves. Here's a classic example: consider a person who is receiving long-term disability payments for depression. To qualify for the payment, they have had to prove how profoundly depressed they are and what a negative impact this is having on their ability to function. This creates the sense that they are defined by their depression, and the expectation that they will be depressed for life. They stop looking for work. They restrict their expectations of themselves. They stagnate and resign themselves to not joining the workforce again. The payment itself, then, can be seen as a secondary gain that has had a negative effect.

Secondary gain is the hidden force that sabotages us and makes us resistant to change and growth. We usually have no idea that this is going on. In this situation, if we had a magical bean to fix our problems, we might not take it because it would mean losing the secondary gains that we get from our problems. If secondary gain is sabotaging our chances of making positive change, we need to recognise it so that we can undo its influence.

CHAPTER 23
ANGER

Anger as a lifestyle is not intelligent. When you have anger as part of your go-to response behaviours, how does that work out for you? In the short term, you can have a vent, you can shift responsibility to people around you as you are busy blaming them for everything, you can tell yourself that other people are the cause of the problem and that they made you angry. You can dominate and bully people to get what you want.

It is not an achievement to intimidate others. Anger is very primitive. We all experience anger, but some of us have learnt to manage our anger, and others have not. If you have skipped this lesson in life, it's time to learn.

But what about the mid- to long-term impacts of anger? If we consistently react with anger, people will figure out that they don't want a relationship and will avoid us. This can be partners, friends, work colleagues, and our children. Why would they want to be around a volatile bully? They have a duty of care to themselves; they need to be surrounded by people they feel emotionally safe with, and who gently nurture them. If we have insight we may then be left with the guilt and regret of pushing our people away. We have created and ignited our own self-destruct mechanism. Even if our partner or adult child is too downtrodden and eroded to separate from us, the quality of the relationship is gone; it is a husk. They are on eggshells. There is a lack of depth, because without emotional safety you cannot have emotional depth. In the mid- to long-term, we isolate ourselves and lose everyone's respect when we have anger issues.

I personally do not have angry people in my life. I won't put up with it. In my personal circle I surround myself with people I can completely breathe out with.

Anger and explosiveness are bad for your physical health also. There is no surprise that anger is linked to heightened blood pressure and heart disease. So, if you have an issue with anger, if anger is your frequent reaction and your go-to in relationships, take it very, very seriously.

Some people enjoy damaging others; they see others as pawns to be played with and dominated. Their goal is not health and happiness; it is drama and destruction. These people are in the psychopathy, sociopathy, narcissistic personality disorder, antisocial personality disorder categories. If you are one of these people, this chapter is not for you, although I doubt very much that you will be reading this anyway. This chapter is rather for the people who are purely reacting with anger out of habit, who experience themselves as frequently erupting volcanoes.

Here is an interesting twist: anger is secondary to sadness and fear. We have primary emotions and secondary emotions. Anger is a secondary emotion and it is really an expression of sadness or fear.

So the question is not 'What are you angry about?'; it is 'What are you sad or fearful about?' Either we are not aware ourselves of what our fear or sad issue is, or we don't want to show these vulnerable emotions because it will make us feel too exposed. Society may have taught you that it is not okay to show this sadness or fear. Many men, for example, are socialised not to cry. They are socialised not to fully express being human. What are they to do then? They bury their feelings of sadness and fear, suppress them, and then react with anger. Anger is purely a mask.

We may feel out of control when things are not going our way. We may have a distorted belief (from our fear of being wrong and vulnerable) that we are routinely right, and that others are wrong. We may be consumed by our own issues and presume how others should respond to our needs. We are fearful and sad that they don't care (even though our expectations are unrealistic), so we rage when they disappoint us. There are innumerable causes of anger. But the real question when we feel angry is this: what are we feeling fearful or sad about? Once we ask this question, then we can start to have an intelligent conversation about the real cause of our anger. We can then actually start to address the issues and stop going in circles, experiencing the same triggers and reactive pattern of anger behaviour over and over again.

CHAPTER 24
HOW DOES ANGER MANAGEMENT WORK?

Anger management is self-regulation of our emotions.

Think about when a child is throwing a tantrum: they are not being a well-behaved version of themselves, so we put them in time-out. After some time in their quiet space, the child decides to calm down because they are bored, and they want to come out and re-join the family. We are teaching them to take responsibility for their emotional state and to choose to calm themselves down. The sooner they calm themselves down, the sooner they are rewarded with freedom.

Anger management is us parenting ourselves. We are extinguishing the volcano within us before it erupts. If we have already erupted, we do not allow the eruption to continue. We put water on our flames. First, we own that *we are responsible* for the escalation of our emotional state and our own volatile behaviour. Even if we are in a situation or with someone who is pressing all of our buttons, *we are responsible* for ourselves and our reaction. Second, we work to catch it as soon as we can. Anger grows, so catch it while it is a small monster, before it grows into a bigger monster. When it is smaller, it is easier to wrestle with, and quicker to recover from.

The next step is to stop engaging with the person or situation that has triggered us. You are not equipped to be constructive when you are angry, so excuse yourself, walk away, put yourself in time-out, and defuse. It is only when you are away from the stressor that you can calm down. This can be difficult, because you have to see what is happening and make the judgement call to walk away – but the real problem is that you *might not want to*. When we are starting to get fired up, we often want to launch, a bit like a dog in attack mode. It is our honest monitoring of this tug-of-war desire to let ourself launch and vent our anger, and the determination not to engage, that is key.

It can be challenging when you are across from someone who is reacting with anger. They may *want* you to engage; they may want the clash, the conflict. Walking away from someone who is fired up and trying to antagonise you is very, very difficult. The positive is that it takes more strength to walk away. You are showing strength by walking away. You are not cowering; you are acting with maturity. You are not bringing yourself down to the level of uncontrolled anger. If this antagonist is your significant other, it can help to tell them this game plan ahead of time, so they understand what you are doing if you walk away from them suddenly. You are defusing your anger bomb. Let them have a chance to understand you and get on board. Otherwise, when you walk away, perhaps say, 'This is not a good time to talk about this. I have to calm down first.'

Once away, see if you can distract your mind to defuse your anger state. Imagine that your mind is like a television; if you change the channel of what you are concentrating on, your emotion has a chance to calm. This distraction needs to be something that engages your mind. Go and do something, build something, create something, clean something, read something, walk, do some stretching, cook. Just watching a screen probably won't cut it, as it is passive and does not engage your brain; you can still think about your angry issue while watching a screen.

A second defusing strategy is journalling, which is a profoundly wonderful tool. Get a pen and notepad and have a verbal and emotional vomit! See it not as a composition but as a release. There are no rules; just let it out. It is for your private eyes only. Keep it, shred it, burn it – whatever works for you. Writing it down not only gives release but also lets us process the issue on a different level. We can get some perspective. We can also see that with time we don't think or feel the same way as when we last journalled. We are able to see time and recovery firsthand.

After we have calmed, we then need to prioritise addressing the problems. Many get over the crisis without going back and working towards fixing the problems, and therefore they recur again and again and again. What are the problems? What do they mean to us? What buttons are being pressed? What do we fear? Is there sadness?

We don't want to repeat the same problems time and time again, so let's work towards understanding, self-knowledge, and knowledge of others. Let's be solution focused.

It is important to communicate a desire to work through the issues with your significant other, negotiate a mutually good time and a good setting, take the time for both of you to write down your agenda, see it as a meeting. This is a quality problem-solving conversation, not conflict. At this meeting you need to use really healthy and constructive skills to get a positive outcome. These skills are covered in depth in Book 4, Chapter 8.

Here's a thought: why do we often control our anger at work and in public, but not at home? Yes, there may be a lot of stressors and triggers at home, but when we get triggered out in the world, we usually do not give free rein to our anger. We reel it in; we control it. We realise that we can't get away with it in the outside world. People would not tolerate it. We would probably get sacked by our boss or our customers. We would be socially ostracised. It is not socially acceptable, so we calm ourselves down and do not launch our anger.

If we can calm our anger at work and in public, this is evidence that we *have* the skills of anger management;

we are just being complacent and letting ourselves go at home. Well, don't. Firstly, our loved ones should be the people that we treat the *best* in our world, and our treatment of them needs to be our basic standard. Secondly, the belief that we can do this at home because they will cop it – that they will still be there for us – is, as stated earlier, naïve and shortsighted. Either they will leave, or the relationship will become damaged and disconnected. We all need to feel safe, and not to walk on eggshells with our lives defined by uncertainty, apprehension and fear.

CHAPTER 25
SELF-FORGIVENESS ...
SELF-COMPASSION

If our world is to keep expanding, we need to learn to deal with our regrets; we need to learn to move on. It is essential for our healing. As well as things we are happy with, we all have things we regret having done or not done. Our job is to learn to move through our regrets and recriminations, as they can lead to inner bitterness. We need to learn to forgive ourselves. This forgiveness involves self-compassion and cultivating love for oneself.

> Learn to forgive yourself,
> again and again and again and again.

The capacity to cultivate compassion and love for ourselves can remedy our sense of fear, stress and feeling overwhelmed. Many of us put caring for ourselves last. We may find being kind and extending compassion to ourselves difficult at first. You may be surprised at how difficult self-forgiveness and self-compassion are. It is usually much easier to forgive others than to forgive ourselves, as our problems with ego and self-identity and our insecurities can all be triggered by our guilt. When we screw up, it can rock us to our core. 'What does this say about who I am as a person?' we might ask.

One of the most important paths to healing is loving ourselves, but unfortunately this is very hard to do for many of us. So much suffering comes from our tendency to be too hard on ourselves. How often do you call yourself a name in your head? 'You're an idiot. You're stupid!' These self-statements are all too common. We would not speak to others the way that we speak to ourselves, so why do we say these things to ourselves? We are being cruel to ourselves and cutting ourselves down.

It is a human condition to be critical of ourselves, judge ourselves day in and day out, to feel unsure of ourselves and lack in confidence. So it is not a stretch to understand why we are routinely poor at self-forgiveness and self-compassion. Practising loving kindness towards yourself is an excellent means of cultivating inner healing. It is a useful antidote. Over time we need to practise greater self-acceptance, and even self-love.

In the process of self-forgiveness, we acknowledge our past and we understand that our past has led us to the present moment. We can usually take a lot of blessings and strengths from this. This is a process of opening our heart to resolution and reconciliation with ourselves. Compassion comes from informed understanding of the complex variables that led us to our actions. This is not excusing our behaviour; this is gently understanding our actions, understanding how our actions were sometimes driven by external pressures, internal insecurities, lack of awareness and fear. Perhaps we understand that historical hot issues are being triggered, or that we are tired, or in a stressful family situation, or have domestic or financial pressures, or health issues – you name it. Perhaps our insecurities have been triggered and we are acting out of fear. Perhaps it is an accumulation of stressors which, if faced separately, would be manageable. Perhaps there is a long history of events that have brought us to our current reactions.

Compassion is about acknowledging the messiness of the factors that contribute to our thoughts, emotions and behaviours. It is about understanding, not judging. It is caring for ourselves as we juggle what is on our plate. This perspective makes us take a step back from pressuring ourselves further. We can be kind and compassionate towards ourselves. We become a helper and supporter for ourselves, rather than torturing ourselves further with negative self-talk.

Another effective approach to help with self-compassion is to step away and see our situation from the outside. We might ask, 'What if a dear friend was in this situation; how would I view it? How would I support them?' We then take that view and support for ourselves. This is self-compassion. With the distance and the lack of personal involvement, we are able to see the situation more objectively and with compassion. We are not filled with self-pressured thoughts that flare up our already stressed situation. For a friend, you can think more clearly about the situation, and respond with kindness, support and encouragement.

Here's an example from my own life. I am a bit of a 'doer'; I am always going from project to project, small or big: building something with the kids, preparing reports, thinking of what would be fun to do next, dealing with domestic stuff, preparing for the next event, writing this book, contacting friends, trying to read too many books. When I am recharged, I am very active. But when I have been pregnant and lacking in energy, I have been terrible at coping with not operating at my usual capacity. I feel frustrated and can get down on myself that I 'should' be at my normal capacity. That's right, the swear word 'should'! I have learnt, however, to respond with a self-compassionate stance. That is, 'If my friend Sarah was as pregnant as me, what would I say to her?' And my answer is a firm, 'You are pregnant; you cannot function as if you are not pregnant. Take it easy, slow down, be realistic, and be kind to yourself.' This is a friend-mode conversation that I needed to have with myself throughout every pregnant and post-pregnant day. I never got to the point where I absorbed it as my own genuine approach. I had to keep *explicitly* having this talk with myself.

We need to untangle what is holding us back from opening our heart to self-compassion and self-forgiveness. We can be great at compassion for our loved ones. We can let our loved ones know that we understand how they feel, that it is fair enough that they feel this way, that they will find a way through, that in time this stress will be behind them. That it will be okay. This is the compassion that we need for ourselves also. Soothe ourselves as we would soothe others. Love ourselves as we would love others. It is only fair and rational.

CHAPTER 26
ACTIVE RECHARGE, NOT PASSIVE (DRAINING) RECHARGE

What do we do with our down time? Do we relax, do we recharge? Actually, it is not that simple. There is **active recharge** and there is **passive recharge**, and the effect of each on us is light-years apart.

Active recharge happens when we engage in leisure pursuits that extend us, our curiosity and our learning; they are meaningful to us and give us a sense of satisfaction. These activities can be learning about something, planning something, reading, sketching, reorganising, doing a hobby, talking with loved ones, going for a walk, relaxing with your feet soaking in warm peppermint water, having a recharging shower or bath. Active recharge is an expression of ourselves, as our choices are unique to us. We may not be challenging ourselves, but we are *doing*; we are extending ourselves.

> *Our nature lies in movement.*
> Blaise Pascal, French philosopher

Passive recharge occurs when you passively engage in leisure. This can be TV, social media, YouTube, gaming etc. (Watching TV is not always a passive drain. An exception is when you watch top-quality comedy that makes you think or belly laugh; or sport that excites you; or documentaries or news shows that expand your mind and make you learn or be amazed.)

With passive recharge, what we might not realise is that when we come away from these things, we actually feel drained of energy and our mood has usually gone down, subtly or noticeably. It should be called 'passive drain', not 'passive recharge'.

We choose TV and social media because we want to zone out from the world. We are killing time and protecting ourselves from our worries. We want to escape. It is a way of self-regulating, just like comfort eating, shopping, taking recreational drugs, drinking, smoking and gambling. Avoiding our worries this way is of course not effective, because when we come back to our conscious world, our worries are still sitting there waiting for us. Plus, with passive recharge, now we feel drained as well. We have nothing to show for all this time we spent in passive recharge. We think that watching TV is our down time, and this might be a reassuring pattern of stimulation, but it can actually make us come away feeling sad, flat, irritable and weakened.

I'm not saying that we should not have 'bludge' TV time, or never flick through social media. I'm saying that we need to *understand* what we're doing and be careful and aware that our energy will actually be depleted, and that we could come away feeling worse, not better. Even if our energy and mood are only subtly worse, they *are* worse. So we need to have our eyes open and moderate ourselves. Flopping in front of the TV or always having our face on a screen is not a lifestyle, and it is not caring for ourselves. It is like using a charger for our phone only to find out that it actually drains the battery, rather than recharges it. We need to know this and then be cautious and sensible.

Of course, social media, with the ping-pong of contact, the constant flow of new information, the comparisons it encourages us to make between ourselves and what we see there, is designed to suck us in. We are like lab rats, and we just keep pressing the lever. So let's be real about just how hard it is to ease off on the social media use. It can be tough.

I have couples who come into my psychology practice with acute relationship difficulties, conflict and disconnection – couples who are teetering on the brink of separation. Routinely, it is apparent that they are investing their time in TV and social media and not in each other. The technology is usually not the foundation cause, but it takes the threads of conflict and disconnect in their relationship and amplifies them so that they end up living on separate islands. They are sucked face-first into the social media epidemic. On questioning, they state that they are desperate for their relationship to work and that they will 'work hard at it', they'll 'try anything', they are 'in', they 'don't want to separate'. So I set them the very essential task of camping for one month. No TV or social media or other screen time. They can only use messaging for the sake of logistics to organise their lives, not for social interaction. The partners then do one of two things. They might refuse – one or both of them. And this shows that they are more committed to this dependent lifestyle than to their relationship. They are married to their social media, not to each other, and it doesn't look good for them. Or they might take time out from the social media rat race and actually turn towards each other and become reacquainted, to have refuelling, reconnecting time – or to listen and learn to understand each other so that they actually can work through their issues. It's not okay to have three in the marital bed, so tech time sometimes needs the boot.

Active recharge requires concentration; it increases skills and leads to the development of the self. It means picking up a book to read instead of putting on the TV. It means researching something, rather than hopping on mind-numbing YouTube and going from clip to clip. In coping with life's anxiety, active recharge leads to growth, while passive recharge is about avoidance and keeping the mind from unravelling. When someone regularly lives in the world of active recharge, they rarely get bored; they are self-sufficient and living a creative life. On the other hand, someone who lives in the world of passive recharge is largely dependent on a screen to stimulate and soothe them.

A great example of the negative effect of passive recharge is shown by the new norm of people having their phones at the dinner table or when socialising. There they are with the real world and real people, but they are not savouring the moment. They are busy pressing the lever of immediate gratification and connecting with the social media world, not their world. Of course, it is extremely rude, but more to the point, it is sad. When we do this, we are not awake to the rich wealth of the world around us. It is at considerable cost to us if we do not wake up from this dependent fog.

The belief that we can be happy and content living through regular passive recharge is foolish and unaware. We cannot avoid the need to live well and grow through extending our strengths of character and pursuing active recharge. Not extending ourselves sets us up for depression. There are no short cuts to living well. We are living in a country that is very fortunate in terms of wealth and standards of living, and yet depression and anxiety and discontent are rising to epidemic levels. We are starving in our sense of confidence, connection and meaning in our lives, and an enormous cause is our passive draining lifestyles.

CHAPTER 27
SLEEP

Sleep is an involuntary process; this is one annoying thing about being human. We are the only creatures who sometimes cannot sleep despite definitely needing to and wanting to. Sleep is a state that we slip into when we are relaxed. If you demand it, it will not come. When we are stressed, we are governed by our sympathetic nervous system (as explained in Book 1) and we can say goodbye to sleep. We need our parasympathetic nervous system to be active if we are to sleep.

When we're stressed, we are of course more likely to wake through the night and, for some, we then cannot go back to sleep. Or perhaps we cannot get to sleep in the first place. In our minds we are turning something over and over, and we are planning or reflecting when we actually need to be in the repair mode of sleep. What's more, this is not usually quality thinking time. We go in circles in our minds, we catastrophise and are overly emotional. We go nowhere trying to settle into sleep.

Sleep is about letting go.

Sleep deprivation is one of the most effective forms of torture, and through our stressed state, this is exactly what we do to ourselves. When we are sleep deprived, our brains do not function, we feel foggy, we cannot think, make decisions, analyse, plan or concentrate. And we lose our sense of humour and might also find we are more reactive – that it's harder to choose our responses.

So, what to do? Here are some suggestions.

1. Obviously the first step is covered earlier with anxiety. Work at learning to control your consciousness; work to address and reduce your anxiety.

2. Have good sleep hygiene. This means no technology one hour before bed, wind your brain down, limit the caffeine after lunch, get rid of light stimulation from technology in your bedroom.

3. Create a sleep routine. Set a sensible bedtime and stick to it. Have a shower, read a book, condition your body to wind down out of habit.

4. Try a heat pack on your neck, shoulders, ankles – wherever feels good. Concentrate on that sensory information, feel your muscles enjoying the warmth and relaxation.

5. Think of the word 'sleep' as a swear word. Do not say it to yourself. Remember, sleep is not something you

can *will* to happen; you must *receive* it. You must leave the concept of sleep alone. Instead, focus on *relaxation*, which is a state that you can control. This then naturally rolls into sleep. Sleep is about letting go.

6. Dedication to breathing techniques is an absolute must. They are your key. I would recommend 'Breathe out for a count of 10' (Book 1, Chapter 39). There are many, many popular relaxation techniques. Quietening your breathing, your heart rate, and your mind is the formula to activate your parasympathetic nervous system, and therefore to slide into sleep.

7. Do not have the television playing when you sleep. Your subconscious will be aware of this stimulation and you will not fully relax and switch off.

8. If you have had a bad night's sleep (including when it is due to waking babies), it is important not to focus on this lost sleep the next day. This focus on sleep missed will just make you feel worse. The next night is a new night; just give it another shot.

9. Get lost in your imagination! The imagination is amazing as a tool to overcome phobias, learn new skills and to utilise the powers of neuroplasticity (the ability of neural networks in the brain to change and rewire themselves). We can use our imagination to carry us to sleep as well. Jump into bed and daydream of an interest that takes your fancy. Immerse yourself

in this daydream state. With enough dedication to this, before you know it, you will drift off to sleep. I really enjoy architecture, so I imagine designing my ultimate house. I walk through it, and it becomes alive in my mind. Clients report to me that they have imagined their ultimate holiday, their ultimate garden, their ultimate gathering with friends, even a sexual fantasy. Wherever your imagination wants to go, let it take you away to your ultimate relaxed state of sleep.

10. Use a technique I call 'socks'. I will explain this below.

SOCKS ...

There is another key technique that works by creating a conditioned response. I call it 'socks'.

We want to condition your body to send itself to sleep because the alternative is unpleasant. Here it is. You go to bed, no clocks in visual range (we do not want you watching the clock). You go to bed at a reasonable time. You lie there for approximately ten minutes (approximate is fine). If you are awake (you will be), then you must get out of bed and walk to a close room where there is a basket of socks. You pair the socks for approximately five minutes. You then go back to bed. You repeat. You go back to bed; in approximately ten minutes if you are not asleep, then up you get and pair socks for five minutes. When the socks are all paired, unpair them again in the basket and then start pairing them again. And repeat, and repeat, and repeat. It sounds crazy, doesn't it? Bed ten minutes, pairing socks five minutes, bed ten minutes, pairing socks five minutes ...

It might seem crazy, but if you are truly sleep deprived, you will try this bizarre technique. And if you follow it diligently, then your body will say, 'For goodness' sake, go to sleep or you will have to get up and pair socks again.' And voilà, you are asleep!

Do this each night and you will notice that you develop a conditioned response. You will not have to get up as many times with each progressive night because the dread of having to get up again makes your body will you to sleep.

This is a gem, and it has worked for literally hundreds of my clients. One caution: this will only work if you have the self-discipline to get yourself up and pair socks every ten minutes of non-sleep time in bed. If you don't have this self-discipline then it won't work. Also, you can do this with children and teenagers if they are willing. If they are young, the parent sits in their room with them and takes them through it. The dedication required for the parent is nothing compared to the usual effort they put into their sleepless child night after night.

CHAPTER 28
DREAMS

One of the rare windows into our unconscious is our dreams. In dreams, our unconscious is knocking on our door, telling us about the issues that are worrying us or that we are working through. While we dream routinely, we only sometimes remember our dreams. Sometimes we are woken during a dream, so we have a sneak look at what we were dreaming the moment before we awoke.

To a psychologist, dreams are precious snapshots of information, as the unconscious is the holy grail of intriguing information. Often it is really valuable information. It is a wonderful exercise to write down what you recall of a dream immediately after you wake up. Have a pen and paper on your bedside table to reach for before your recollection floats away. Write down as much detail as you can. This practice might help you learn to remember your dreams more frequently and vividly. Dreams are not just weird; they are full of information about you and how your mind works.

Dreams do not speak our language; they are not literal. Dreams speak in images, stories and symbols, and they require interpretation. Since your dreams are all about *you*, your dreams are about what the objects mean to you.

What does that location tell you about yourself? What does that object tell you about yourself? What does that person tell you about yourself? What do they represent? These questions are the art of interpreting dreams. This is dream language for you to disentangle. You are represented in these different images, stories and symbols. If there is a scary figure, it is about the part of you that feels fear. If your dream is about facing a threat or a challenge, the dream is about the courageous part of you. With this information we can visit our vulnerabilities and our aspirations and be more real with and informed about ourselves.

Dreams offer questions and perspectives, not usually answers. Often, however, seeing the new perspective gives you a clear-thinking pathway to the answer. For example, I recall a clear dream where I told a friend some bad news, and my friend grew into an enormous beast and raged with protest, trying to intimidate me. This dream was strangely not scary; it just showed me that I distrusted this person. This dream empowered me into action. It was telling me that I did not feel safe with this person; that I knew this person was volatile. As it played out, I did indeed feel safer when I chose to distance myself from them.

Symbols can be tricky and are up for subjective interpretation. Again, it is a case of what the symbol represents to you. Pay attention to dreams that might be flagging to you that you may have a physical illness. Take the hint and get it medically checked out. You can thank your unconscious later if it was a good tip-off.

CHAPTER 29
HORMONES – TAME THE DRAGON

Women, let's talk hormones. Let's talk pre-menstrual tension. It can take years to learn to 'ride the dragon', your hormonal mood. We need to learn to steer our dragon rather than to be dragged along by it. We can be hijacked by our hormones, and our emotional state can become heightened to needlepoint, piercing through our usual rational selves. The best we can do is own it, call it, let loved ones know that we are feeling a bit vulnerable, that we need some space and we are going to be functioning on skeleton staff for a while. If we can be real with it, we can create distance between our immediate reactions and how we usually allow ourselves to respond. We take responsibility for our reactive behaviour even though it is not the usual us.

If you really have extreme emotional volatility when you are premenstrual, then you may have premenstrual dysphoric disorder. This is the severe, *severe* end of the spectrum, and if this is where you are, then you might need antidepressants. Relationships can be damaged when we don't ensure that our standards for treating others remain really high, no matter what. If you are at risk of doing damage to others and yourself, throwing dragon grenades, then you should probably chat with your doctor. Even if it is not so severe, you might wish to explore options or therapies to regulate your hormones so you do not experience the intensity so much in the first place.

CHAPTER 30
ENERGY TOWARDS OTHERS

What energy to you radiate out to others? Positive people attract positive people, and negativity radiates out to others. Each and every moment we need to mould and shape our energy through our control of our consciousness. How we live our life, with our thoughts, feelings, beliefs and values affects the energy that we extend within ourselves and out towards others. When we feel joyful, delighted and excited, we draw more positive responses from others, such as smiles, laughter, and lightness. We can improve others' moods and experiences. When we feel fearful and anxious, we will selectively notice the negative things around us and absorb this. People will respond with apprehension and wariness around us when we radiate negative energy.

You have the potential to be a tremendously energetic and powerful being. Maybe you already are. Maybe you demonstrate how we can embrace possibilities and open our minds to the world. You are a curious student of the world. You can continue to grow, and your joy grows as your world expands. Are you bouncing in life or deflated?

Who are the people, what are the projects around you that are fuelling your energy? There is power and energy in you. You just need to learn to master it. We need more happiness in the world. Be part of it.

IN CONCLUSION

So many of the concepts and judgements that we take for granted are gross distortions of reality. The world we *think* we see is merely the projection of a set of rules that we've made for ourselves. Until we shake up this way of seeing the world, we can feel empty, question ourselves and our purpose, and wonder why we're here. We can deny the world's loveliness. The great news is that we have the freedom to wake up if we just know where to look. To do this we need a whole new lens for looking at ourselves and our world. We need to peel back what is inconsequential, what is distracting and what is trivial, so that we are left with what is valuable in life.

As we create this informed new lens, we come to see *ourselves* with more compassion and understanding. We discover our core values, our passions and our purpose. We become far clearer about what makes life meaningful for us. This level of self-awareness and healthy functioning will then have a ripple effect to incorporate our connection with others, allowing us to develop deeper and more genuine relationships.

FURTHER READING

The works on attachment by Ainsworth and Bowlby that I referred to are listed below. If you wish to read more on some of the topics raised in this book, try the works of John O'Donohue. He shares soothing and reassuring prose that resonates with the challenging path to learning about ourselves.

Ainsworth, M (1978), *Patterns of attachment: a psychological study of the strange situation*, Halstead Press Division of Wiley, New York.

Bowlby, J (1979), *Making and breaking of affectionate bonds*, Tavistock Publication, London.

O'Donohue, J (1997), *Anam Cara: a book of Celtic wisdom*, Harper Perennial, New York.

O'Donohue, J (2005), *Beauty: the invisible embrace*, Harper Perennial, New York.

O'Donohue, J (2008), *To bless the space between us: a book of blessings*, Doubleday, New York.

And, finally, if you wish to explore the topics I have touched on briefly in this book more deeply, you might like to try the other books in the 'Signposts for Living' series by Dr Kirsten Hunter:

Book 1: Control your Consciousness – In the Driver's Seat

Book 3: Mindfulness and State of Flow – Living with Purpose and Passion

Book 4: Understanding Others – Loved Ones to Tricky Ones

Book 5: Parenting – Love, Pride, Apprenticeship

Book 6: Nailing Being an Adult – Have the Skills

ACKNOWLEDGEMENTS

To Jon, my beautiful husband, your support is constant. I can always rely on you to be in my corner, patiently championing me on while I sit typing away. With writing, having someone who believes in you makes all the difference. Thank you that it is always 'us' facing the next challenge, the next hurdle. I love you.

My devoted mum has been the rock through my childhood and every chapter of my adulthood. No child could have a more extraordinary mum. I'm proud of you and I love you.

Our five boys, Lachlan, James, Tobias, Jack, and George, when you heard that your mum was writing books, non-fiction and fiction, your response was simply 'of course she is'. When you heard mum was publishing, your response was 'of course she is'. When we talk about the book being successful in reaching a wide audience, your response, 'of course it will'. You boys are so beautiful. Ever-resounding support, thank you. I love you.

Vanya Lowther, you are the smartest person I know, and perhaps the wisest. You are also my closest and my lifelong friend. Thank you for taking on the mammoth task of being the first person to put your eyes on the *Signposts for Living* books. Your perseverance, your contribution and brainpower was and is so appreciated. I love you.

Jane Smith, I agree with Stephen King, 'to write is human, to edit is divine'. Thank you for your eye for detail, your grammatical wizardry and staying fresh when there was so much work to do. You're a talented gem.

ABOUT THE AUTHOR

Dr Kirsten Hunter is a clinical psychologist with 20 years' experience working with children, adolescents, adults, and couples across the expanse of clinical areas. Between running her private practice, enjoying time with her family, and writing her books, Kirsten juggles a range of passions – particularly for scuba diving and hiking. Kirsten is known for diving deep into life, creating and embracing all of life's opportunities. Born in Brisbane, she now lives in Toowoomba, Australia, with her six men: her husband and their five sons. Even their pets are male ...